Praise for Church for the Fatherless

"Dr. Mark Strong is a man of faith who is also firmly rooted in the real world. That makes him the perfect messenger. This book gets to the heart of an issue that remains one of the most challenging in our society. Dr. Strong's book is uplifting and filled with hope. But it also fosters a conversation that needs to take place. To read his words is to have Dr. Strong sitting next to you and engaging you in a thoughtful discussion. That is a gift and a pleasure."

TOM HALLMAN JR., Pulitzer Prize winner and author of *Sam: The Boy Behind the Mask*

"More and more pastors deal with the reality of fatherlessness in our community. Mark Strong's timely work presents honest and real insight that challenges the church to live into our calling to foster fatherhood to the fatherless. Strong offers practical and helpful ministry solutions for the important work of healing and redemption."

SOONG-CHAN RAH, associate professor of church growth and evangelism, North Park Theological Seminary, author of *The Next Evangelicalism*

"Mark Strong doesn't just unveil the hidden horrors of fatherlessness—he shows how to turn its hardening of hearts into a gardening of hearts."

LEONARD SWEET, bestselling author and professor at Drew University

"Mark Strong is a true father and pastor. Over the years that I have known him, I have always admired his unique mix of strength and gentleness. The passion to protect and restore hurting people that is so evident is his ministry shines clearly through this book. I believe his call to the church to become fathers to the fatherless is as timely as it is powerful."

JUDAH SMITH, lead pastor of The City Church, Seattle

"Fatherlessness has become an epidemic in America. The church needs to wake up to this crisis. In *Church for the Fatherless,* pastor-evangelist Mark Strong provides a how-to manual to help mobilize churches to stop the epidemic and mentor those devastated by this critical issue. . . . Mark shows how the faith-based community, working together, can provide hope to the fatherless."

KEVIN PALAU, president, Luis Palau Association

"What I found most compelling was Pastor Strong's use of story. He invites you into the lives of real people and provides insight into how we can practically invest our lives in helping the fatherless—one child at a time. His book is hopeful, always resting on the work of the Holy Spirit empowering his people to be agents of love in this world."

ROBIN BAKER, president, George Fox University

"With skill, sensitivity and the Scriptures, Pastor Strong leads us to face the issue of fatherlessness and what it means for now and the future. While this book is an honest assessment of the issue, it is not without hope or answers, and the compassion with which fatherlessness is dealt with makes it a book anyone can read and not feel condemned. I grew up in a home without my dad and I know the ache that such reality leaves. Thank God that there is hope, and this book tells us how to find it. Read it and be blessed, read it and be changed."

BISHOP TIMOTHY J. CLARKE, First Church of God, Columbus, Ohio

"Pastor Mark Strong is a bright light of hope in his city and community. He has genuinely lived the message of this book and has become a healing power to the fatherless generation. . . . If we embrace the insights in this book, we would impact thousands of lives and change the culture of the fatherless. This book is a must-read and an inspiration to all of us to get off the bench and into the game."

DR. FRANK DAMAZIO, lead pastor, City Bible Church, and chairman, Ministers Fellowship International

"Compelling, urgent, a must-read for those who care about the church and families. Fatherlessness is a national tragedy resulting in layer upon layer of social and emotional ills. Pastor Strong's call for the church to be God's redemptive agent to the fatherless, along with his passion, experience and practical solutions, inspires hope that every child might know a father's blessing."

MARYKATE MORSE, author of Making Room for Leadership

"Pastor Mark Strong practices what he preaches and teaches on fathering the fatherless. He and his church are serving as a catalytic force as they partner with others to address the growing crisis of fatherlessness in our city of Portland with love, mercy and faithfulness. You will be more strategically prepared to care for the orphans in distress in your own community as you take to heart the prophetic and practical wisdom of this critically important volume."

PAUL LOUIS METZGER, Ph.D., professor, Multnomah Biblical Seminary

CHURCH FOR THE FATHERLESS

A MINISTRY MODEL FOR
SOCIETY'S MOST PRESSING PROBLEM

MARK E. STRONG

IVP Books

An imprint of InterVarsity Press
Downers Grove, Illinois

InterVarsity Press
P.O. Box 1400, Downers Grove, IL 60515-1426
World Wide Web: www.ivpress.com
E-mail: email@ivpress.com

InterVarsity Press® is the book-publishing division of InterVarsity Christian Fellowship/USA®, a
movement of students and faculty active on campus at hundreds of universities, colleges and schools
of nursing in the United States of America, and a member movement of the International Fellowship
of Evangelical Students. For information about local and regional activities, write Public Relations
Dept., InterVarsity Christian Fellowship/USA, 6400 Schroeder Rd., P.O. Box 7895, Madison, WI
53707-7895, or visit the IVCF website at <www.intervarsity.org>.

All Scripture quotations, unless otherwise indicated, are taken from THE HOLY BIBLE, NEW
INTERNATIONAL VERSION®, NIV® Copyright © 1973, 1978, 1984, 2011 by Biblica, Inc.™ Used
by permission. All rights reserved worldwide.

While all stories in this book are true, some names and identifying information in this book have
been changed to protect the privacy of the individuals involved.

Cover design: Cindy Kiple
Images: torn paper: © spxChrome/iStockphoto
        silhouette of a man: © Clayton Bastiani/Trevillion Images
        silhouette mug shots: Leontura/iStockphoto
Interior design: Beth Hagenberg

ISBN 978-0-8308-3790-8

Printed in the United States of America ∞

Library of Congress Cataloging-in-Publication Data has been requested.

P	18	17	16	15	14	13	12	11	10	9	8	7	6	5	4	3	2	1
Y	27	26	25	24	23	22	21	20	19	18	17	16	15	14	13	12		

To

Dad & Mom
(Luther Jr. & Jessie B. Strong)

Nana & Papa
(James & Margaret [deceased] Crolley)

CONTENTS

INTRODUCTION

When we first purchased the old, dilapidated grocery store that would become our new church, a number of the leaders in our church gathered for a prayer in the center of the dark shell laced with mold, undesirable creatures and odors not for man or beast. We formed a large circle and began to pray for God's blessing on the project. As we were praying, for some reason unknown to me, I began to look around at the people who stood praying. It wasn't as if I were looking at strangers; I knew all these people well—many I had known for years. Some were in their twenties, some in their thirties, some in their forties, fifties and sixties. Some were white and some were black.

However, in that moment I was keenly made aware of a shared issue among many of the people in our group. I let my gaze travel around the circle, person by person and one by one, muttering in my mind the phrase "no father, no father, no father . . . "

Approximately fifteen out of the twenty or so individuals in our meeting that night had grown up without an active paternal presence. How can this be? What is happening in our culture to create such a situation?

Defining the Problem

Gone are the days when it was "normal" for a child to grow up with both parents in the home. The idea of a child having the benefit of being reared by a mother and a father together has become a figment of an imagination rooted in antiquity. Equally distressing is that the father is the parent who is generally missing in action—the one abandoning the children. David Blankenhorn, founder of Institute for American Values, makes this observation:

> The United States is becoming an increasingly fatherless so-
> ciety. A generation ago, an American child could reasonably
> expect to grow up with his or her father. Today, an American
> child can reasonably expect not to. . . . Tonight, about 40
> percent of American children will go to sleep in homes in
> which their fathers do not live. Before they reach the age of
> eighteen, more than half of our nation's children are likely to
> spend a significant portion of their childhoods living apart
> from their fathers. Never before in this country have so many
> children been voluntarily abandoned by their fathers. Never
> before have so many children grown up without knowing
> what it means to have a father.[1]

Between 1960 and 1990, the percentage of children living apart from their father rose from 17 to 36, and it continues to rise.[2] Father absenteeism is rising to troubling and problematic propor-tions in our day.

In the African American community, the fatherless plight is worse. The 1990 U.S. Census reported that 48.5 percent of African American homes are headed by single mothers.[3] Poverty and crime are just two of the social ills fueled by father absenteeism in communities across our nations.

Statistics have a tendency to be sterile and impersonal. However, this issue rips at my heart. I have witnessed the tragedy of father absenteeism. I have seen it in my own family. I have also witnessed it firsthand in my church. For over twenty-four years, I have ministered to countless individuals in an urban context— children, teens and adults of all ethnic groups and socioeconomic backgrounds—who have lived most of their lives without a father or with an inadequate father. While some people affected by fatherlessness have adjusted and are healthy and whole, many struggle to deal with issues inherent in fatherlessness.

The story of four-year-old Christopher comes to mind. He was standing outside the door of the church while his grandmother was inside serving people who needed clothes or bread. As he stood there on the curb, enjoying the sunshine, waiting for Granny to finish, a strange man rode up on a bike and began to talk to him. The stranger asked Christopher, "Do you know who I am?" With childlike honesty, Christopher said, "I don't know who you are." To which the stranger replied, "I'm your blood daddy."

Blood daddy? Christopher was thinking, *What in the world is a blood daddy?*

The strangeness of the man's response prompted Christopher to call for his grandmother: "Grandma, you need to come outside. There is a man out here who says he's my blood daddy." When his grandmother stepped out the door, sure enough, she saw it was his biological father. She greeted him, and he took five dollars out of his pocket and gave it to Christopher. He promised he would come by to visit him. Years have passed, and the blood daddy hasn't kept that promise.

Fathering Skills

Physical presence isn't the only issue related to fathers; adequacy is just as important.[4] *Adequacy* refers to the skills a man needs to be a competent father. In my experience at our church, a father's influence in the home is sometimes detrimental to his children's welfare. Such cases usually involve an abusive man with an unhealthy need to exert dictatorial control over his family or an ignorant man who believes that just because he's a man, he has the God-given right to do as he pleases.

I will never forget a conversation I had with a young woman who attended our church. She had recently married the young man who had fathered her child. The marriage lasted only a short time, and the two decided to share custody of their young son. The little boy had just returned home to his mom after spending several weeks with his dad. Upon his return, he began to call his mom and other women derogatory names, and then stated his desire to be a pimp like his daddy. What behavior had this father been exhibiting around his son? While this man was present physically, his influence instilled negative and antisocial behaviors in his son. A father must not only be present, but must also be equipped with the necessary skills to act appropriately as a father to the child. Otherwise, he can do more harm than good.

Being a good father requires having a good fathering skill set, including the right temperament. A father should be loving and merciful to his children, not harsh or overbearing. In addition, a dad should have the ability to teach his children about life and God. A father is on the frontlines when it comes to equipping his children to live and to function effectively in society. Fathers should also possess the skills to provide discipline and correction to their children in a way that doesn't destroy the child, but aids the child in having correct behavior, perspective and attitude. Fathers also need to live in an exemplary fashion so their children have a model to emulate. They also need skills to have a good marriage, because the health of a marriage affects the health of the child.

The Role of the Church

I believe every child has the right to experience the blessing of a father in some fashion. In fact, I believe every child has an innate desire to have a good father as well.

I remember an old song by the Temptations, "Papa Was a

Rolling Stone." The dagger in the song is in the last line of the chorus: "When he died, all he left us was alone." According to statistical trends and my personal experience, too many children are being left alone. In communities throughout America and the world, the odds are stacked against our youth and children.

Too many children are fatherless, and the church—as God's redemptive agent in the community—has a responsibility to address this issue. The fatherless void has created a vortex that is pulling our children and youth into a place of pain, hardship and vulnerability to a destructive lifestyle. If churches, ministries and organizations will engage in a small way by addressing the fatherless problem, our children will have a greater chance to avoid becoming sad statistics. They also will have a greater chance of becoming dedicated disciples of the Lord Jesus Christ.

The quest of this book is threefold. First, I want to help you as a pastor or a leader gain a deeper understanding of the problems surrounding the issue of fatherlessness. Second, I want to share some practical and doable ways your church, ministry or organization can serve the fatherless. Third, I want to inspire and encourage you to engage in and be a part of God's answer to fill the fatherless void. Together in Christ we can address this critical problem in the lives of the fatherless.

We must understand as the church that ministry to the fatherless is not simply an option. It's a biblical mandate and charge we are to follow. The Bible teaches us that God himself is our good, loving Father who is intimately connected and involved in the lives of his children. In Psalm 68:5, God is called "a father to the fatherless." In the Old Testament alone, over forty Scriptures make ministry to the fatherless a priority and a matter of justice for the Israelite community.

The same is true in the New Testament. James poignantly tells us that the true litmus test that validates our religion is our response to orphans and widows: "Religion that God our Father accepts as pure and faultless is this: to look after orphans and widows in their distress and to keep oneself from being polluted by the world" (Jas 1:27). Therefore, from a biblical perspective, we have a God-mandated responsibility as the church to minister to the fatherless. The Bible clearly expresses to us God's heart for all children to experience the life-giving support of either a biological or a surrogate father.

Essential to addressing any problem effectively is the need to understand the issue. To help us gain a cursory understanding, the next two chapters will focus on the causes of fatherlessness and the enormous impact it has on lives. Statistically, the African American community has been hit the hardest by the fatherless plight. That being the case, necessary attention will be given to aid in creating a solution. However, the discussion is not limited to a single ethnic group. The reason being, the fatherless problem is colorless: rich, poor, white, black, brown, yellow and red are all affected.

Part two of the book gives doable strategies that are applicable for any church, regardless of its size and demographic composition and regardless of it being a suburban, rural or urban community.

The church of Jesus Christ is one. Together, in our God-given uniqueness, through him we all can and will make a difference in the lives of the fatherless. The heart of this author is to help the fatherless, no matter the color of their skin.

PART ONE

Understanding
the Problem

1

FATHER, WHERE ARE YOU?

Some time ago, _Newsweek_ magazine featured an article titled "Father, Where Art Thou?" The picture above the title showed a teenager in jail garb. Just inches from his acne-blotched cheek was the shoulder of an officer bearing the seal of Fairfax County Corrections. The following page included a picture of the first Beltway bullet fired by seventeen-year-old sniper Lee Malvo. Malvo was on trial for the sniper shootings of twenty-one people and the death of fourteen in six states. Those two pictures alone ask a troubling question: what would drive a young man with all his life before him to choose to destroy himself and the lives of others?

Malvo's actions may have a number of plausible explanations. His aunt, Marie Lawrence, articulated one explanation that carried considerable weight: she believed her family was cursed. The curse, however, was not a hex or some sort of incantation, but the absence of fathers. She said, "We don't know what is father love."

As a boy, Malvo was abandoned by his father, just as his mother was abandoned by her father. In addition, his mother left him to survive on his own at times while she went to search for a better life in other cities. At age fourteen, he was left in Antigua in an old shack while his mother went to Florida in search of the American Dream.

During her absence, the landlord cut off the electricity in the shack, and Malvo was left alone in those four walls with anger and frustration no child should have to bear. In that state of mind, he began to attach himself to John Allen Muhammad—a lethal father figure—and the rest of the tragic story is history. Muhammad filled the father void for Malvo and led him down a road that no loving father would ever choose.[1]

While not all fatherless children go to these violent extremes, the truth remains that children long for and need the influence of a father. Unfortunately, some seek to fill the void in ways that result in their own detriment.

A few thousand years ago, Malachi the prophet penned a statement that is applicable to the fatherless climate of our day. Speaking of John the Baptist, the forerunner of Christ, he wrote, "He will turn the hearts of the fathers to their children, and the hearts of the children to their fathers; or else I will come and strike the land with a curse" (Mal 4:6). Without discussing all the theological nuances and implications of this verse, I simply want to stress that the prophet identified a disconnection between fathers and children and implied that it would have harmful repercussions.

We are currently experiencing a disconnection between fathers and children in dramatic portions. The questions we must ask ourselves are, Why are nearly half of the children in our nation going to bed at night without a father in their lives? If you had asked these questions fifty years ago, the answers might have been a bit simpler, because the major cause of father absenteeism was death, not a myriad of other factors.[2] However, times have changed, our culture has changed, values have changed and the political landscape has changed. In this chapter we'll examine the major causes of father absenteeism to help us understand the fuel that feeds the fire of fatherlessness in our society.

A Historical Cause: World War II

Quoting Ernest Burgess, scholar Donna Franklin states, "So comprehensive and fundamental are the changes brought by war, and so closely is the family interrelated with the larger society, that perhaps there is no aspect of family life unaffected by war."[3] In the eyes of many sociologists, World War II greatly impacted American culture and placed a great amount of stress and tension on families. Franklin stresses this point:

> World War II had a profound effect on American society. For the United States, it lasted twice as long as World War I, brought over fourteen million men and women into the armed forces, and added another ten million to the labor force. Family life considered an institution began a period of significant change. Arthur Marwick has argued, war always tests existing institutions, and sometimes leads to their transformation or collapse.[4]

World War II did indeed bring change to the American family and in many ways collapse as well. The war altered and in some cases permanently changed the lives of twenty-four million people directly and millions of other people indirectly. Unlike the Vietnam War, during which everyone *knew* of a family who had someone in the war, during World War II, every family *had* someone in the war.

While I don't necessarily buy into the *Ozzie and Harriet* or *Brady Bunch* view of marriage and family, I do believe it is good to have both Mom and Dad in the house. How they work out the roles is up to them; however, both need to be close enough to be lovingly accessible to the children and to one to another. When a parent is absent, something is lost that can be very hard to find again.

World War II ripped the heart out of the family ideal by separating mothers from their children, husbands from their wives and fathers from their children. Mothers were forced to work and in many instances to spend long hours away from the family. The percentage of working women rose from 17 in the 1930s to 25 by the end of the war.[5] This meant that while Dad was off fighting, Mom was off working in the shipyard. During this time, opportunities opened up for many teens and youths to enter the labor force. It's interesting that juvenile crimes rose to the highest level during this period.[6]

At the beginning of the war, military leaders did not favor drafting fathers. The rationale for this was that every child needed and deserved to have the blessing of a father in the home. However, by 1943 it was deemed necessary to draft fathers because quotas could not be filled with single men and men without children. This ruling brought a considerable amount of protest. In his book *Fatherless America,* David Blankenhorn writes,

> Popular opinion remained decisively opposed to drafting fathers. A Gallup poll during the fall of 1943 found that 68 percent of Americans believed that compared to drafting fathers, it was preferable to draft single men employed in industries essential to the war effort. Public opinion also favored drafting single women for noncombat military service to avoid drafting fathers. As George Gallup put it, the public objected to the father draft because it would break up too many families where there are children.[7]

The public was right. It's estimated that three to four million fathers were killed in combat, and many others returned home as frustrated, angry men never able to readjust to family life. Others who made it out alive remained absent from their families for months and years.[8]

World War II not only affected the family structure of white America, but also had adverse effects on African American families. In her book *Ensuring Inequality,* Donna Franklin points out several ways she believes the war hurt black families. One such way was the sudden and late northern migration to urban sprawls.

> World War II placed severe strains on all American families, but its heaviest impact was felt by the African American family, weakened by slavery, share-cropping and the northern migration. During the 1940s, twice the number of blacks migrated to the North than had relocated between 1910 and 1930. By the end of the postwar decade, the proportion of blacks in urban areas would finally exceed those in rural areas—a shift that had been made by whites some thirty years before.[9]

As African Americans made the trek northward, they encountered obstacles that affected their families. The first was a lack of housing. The government attempted to rectify the situation, but failed miserably. The majority of its attempts were aimed at white communities, and when it tried to develop housing for blacks, it was met with strong resistance from whites. It goes without saying, it's hard to raise a family without a roof over your head.[10]

Franklin also points out that blacks were thirty years late in their migration. In my family, when you were late for dinner, you were privileged to eat the leftovers. By the time blacks made the northern migration, there were not many leftovers available, as whites had had a thirty-year head start. The reality of slim resources, complicated by racism, made this harsh transition doubly difficult. Franklin points out the effect of poverty on the family life of blacks:

> Facing a weakened economy without the social controls that once provided communal aspects of the southern life, black marriages disintegrated and out of wedlock births proliferated, especially among adolescents. Although clearly dissatisfied in their competition with white women for jobs in

the labor market, many black women opted not to return to the paltry wages and irregular hours of the domestic service jobs they had before the war. In an effort to cope with their much higher desertion, separation and divorce from black men, and with the difficulty of securing support from the financially beleaguered fathers, black mothers became more reliant on welfare.[11]

My grandmother tells of migrating from Oklahoma to Portland. In Oklahoma the job opportunities were scarce. Most of the jobs available to blacks at the time were hotel clerk positions, stocking jobs in markets, house cleaning, nanny jobs and other menial labor positions. It was difficult for my grandfather to support his family with the slim opportunities present. Being a black man in the Depression era and during a world war complicated the situation even more.

In 1943 my grandfather was forced to move northward. Leaving my grandmother, my dad and my uncle, he went to Portland in search of a way to support his family. Upon arriving in Portland, Gramps encountered discrimination on many levels, but fortunately was able to land a job at the shipyard. Our story turned out fine, but as Grandma says, "It was good but difficult." For some families, things were difficult and things did not turn out so fine.

While economic hardships alone can't be blamed for the deterioration of black families in the World War II era, the impact of poverty can't be denied. After the war, fathers couldn't find jobs, and mothers were forced to take the lower-paying domestic jobs that whites refused to take. This produced a situation detrimental to African American families. Economic inequality helped to grease the slide toward divorces, births to unwed mothers and reliance on welfare. In the end, the mother was often left with the children while the father was left to struggle to make a living.

Voluntary Father Absenteeism

Unlike soldiers whose absence from their families was mandatory during World War II, men today are leaving or abandoning their children voluntarily. Studies in the 1990s demonstrated that never before had so many fathers willingly left their children. Many men left their homes and never glanced back.[12]

A man in our church told me what happened shortly after he was born. His father walked out of the home and deserted him, his mother and the rest of his siblings. I asked him if his father ever tried to contact the family or to help out in any fashion. His answer was an emphatic "No!" He went on to say, "He did nothing at all. When he was gone, he was gone." Sadly, though the characters and places may change, this father act has become commonplace.

Blankenhorn points out several interesting statistics about volitional abandonment. He says that historically the primary cause of father absenteeism was paternal death: "By the time they turned fifteen, about 15 percent of all American children born in 1870 had experienced the death of their fathers. Only slightly more than half reached 15 with both parents still alive."[13]

Due to medical and technological advancements, parents are living longer today. Though death has historically been the primary culprit of father absenteeism, it has been eclipsed by voluntary abandonment. Blankenhorn writes that now more marriages end in divorce than in death.[14]

Blankenhorn believes that from a child-development and social perspective, voluntary abandonment is more difficult to cope with than paternal death. His rationale is as follows:

1. When a child's father dies, a child can properly grieve. The child can eventually (as painful as it may be) come to understand that death is final.

2. When a father leaves, it creates a plethora of psycho-

logical ramifications for the child (self-blame, anxiety, resentment, etc.).

3. When a father dies, fatherhood lives on in the head and the heart of the child, and the legacy of fatherhood is preserved. The mother generally aids in this process of preservation.

4. When a father leaves, the child suffers, and his fatherhood is diminished and the value of fatherhood as a whole suffers. In many cases, because the mother is hurt, she aids in the diminishing process.[15]

The other day I saw two television shows: *Home Improvement* and *That's So Raven*. In the first, a construction team remodeled the house of a needy family; the father had died the previous year due to a terminal illness. The other program was about a young woman who had engaged the help of her friends to keep a friend's parents from getting a divorce. Each of these programs dealt with father issues related to voluntary and involuntary absenteeism.

What's interesting is the way the children responded to the different types of father absenteeism. In the *Home Improvement* program, the children were obviously deeply sorrowful over the loss of their dad. However, when they talked about their father, there was no self-blame or anxiety. The statements they made were, "I know my dad loves us and he is with us and watching over us." The statements were laced with sorrow and longing for their dad, but were positive in nature.

In *That's So Raven*, a teenage boy who was trying to keep his friend's arguing parents from divorcing made several comments that reflected the pain many children feel when a parent walks out. For example, he said, "You gotta try harder so your parents won't split up" and "You must do what you can to keep it from happening." At the end of the program, Raven tells the friend, "It's not your fault your parents split up. You have to stop blaming yourself." The boy replies, "Yeah," lowers his head and walks out the door.

One might think that the biological connection would be enough to keep fathers from voluntarily abandoning their children. According to researchers Wade Horn and Tom Slyvester, "Among teens, only 67 percent live with their biological fathers, compared with the 91 percent who live with their biological mothers. In urban areas, the percentage of teens who live with their fathers drops to only 57 percent."[16] While mothers typically will not leave their children under any circumstances, 24.7 million children live in America without their biological father.[17]

A lot of different factors contribute to the problem of voluntary absenteeism on the part of fathers. Here are several of those factors:

- Employment issues
- Dysfunctional relationship with the child's mother
- Addiction
- Welfare policies
- No commitment to marriage
- Life frustration
- Generational patterns (leaving my children like my dad left me)
- Selfishness

. . . and the list goes on.

The Media

A few years back, my wife and I were watching *The Practice* on television. Part of the storyline involved a young female attorney, Eleanor, who decided she wanted to have a baby. After much consideration, she asked a male friend she admired to be a sperm donor for her child. She chose the man because she valued his character, intelligence and demeanor. Her friend consented, and she was impregnated.

When the office staff received the news of her pregnancy, most everyone was excited. The only person who failed to congratulate her was her close friend Jimmy. She pulled Jimmy aside and asked him why he wasn't happy for her like everyone else. He replied, "I think the baby needs a daddy." Eleanor proceeded to tell him how disappointed she was in him for his failure to support her decision. Finally he congratulated her because of their friendship. He was the only person to object during the whole episode.

When the child was born, the father's conscience convicted him, and he desperately wanted to become a part of the child's life. Eleanor vehemently refused, and off to court they went. The dad pleaded and begged, but he lost because he had signed a contract prior to the pregnancy that forfeited all his paternal rights.

This is just one example of how our media tend to portray fathers as less than central to the parenting process. Jonetta Rose Barras, in her book *Whatever Happened to Daddy's Little Girl?* writes, "Our culture's decision-making created the mythology of the superfluous father."[18] Myths are powerful and can create reality, as in the case of the irrelevancy of the father in our American culture. The myth of the "useless father" presents a unique challenge to the notion that all children need their father.

This challenge to fatherhood is also found in some of the values and messages conveyed through the media and entertainment world. In her book *Media Effects and Society*, Elizabeth Perse highlights two functions of mass media: to project our existing cultural values and to teach these values to others. While no single television program can harness the value system of an entire culture, it can speak to certain aspects.[19]

In 1992, the television character Murphy Brown dropped a bombshell when she decided to mother a child without the involvement of a father. This show prompted Dan Quayle's controversial "Murphy Brown" speech, in which he castigated a culture that promotes fatherhood as "irrelevant."[20] Two years later, continuing on the same theme in a speech titled "Standing Firm,"

Quayle stated, "A society that promotes the idea that a father's role is irrelevant breeds irresponsibility."[21]

The CBS show *60 Minutes* interviewed singer Mellissa Etheridge and her partner Julie Cypher. They had given birth to two children through a sperm donor. The carrot of the show was that they were going to reveal the sperm donor's identity. The donor turned out to be David Crosby of the folk rock group Crosby, Stills and Nash. He had no problem at all with the arrangement. The tone and message of the program seemed to be, "Out with the traditional models of family; do what seems right for you, and everything will work out great. If you desire to have a child without a father being an active part of the child's life, that's totally acceptable."

"I do not believe that my children will be wanting in any way because they didn't have a father in the home every single day," Etheridge said. "What they have in the home is two loving parents. I think that puts them ahead of the game."[22] Though this ideology is not embraced by everyone in our culture, it's definitely present in the media, and it does have an impact on the number of children who have fathers actively involved in their lives.

The Decline of Marriage

Marriage has fallen on hard times. People are now marrying later in life or not at all. Some feel that marriage is simply one option among many for a relationship that may produce children. No one would contest the assertion that marriage is far less important in our culture than it used to be. According to Maggie Gallagher, this is significant to the lives of children. In *Lost Fathers* she writes,

> Marriage is the vehicle by which, throughout history, society creates ties between men and their children. The current fumbling that attempts to produce these ties outside of marriage is without precedent and unlikely to succeed for the simple reason that marriage and parenting are not, as the

experts have imagined, job labels that can be transferred from one employee to the next as personnel shift, but something else entirely: erotic relationships.[23]

In my pastoral ministry, I have observed father participation in the lives of children in married and non-married situations. During my twenty-plus years as pastor of Life Change Christian Center, we have had only a few single fathers in our church who were raising their children on their own. In each case, the father had one child, and the dads had help from the mothers at times. On the other hand, we have seen numerous single mothers who have raised one to five children on their own without the help of a father. The biological tie alone is not enough to keep a father actively involved in the life of his kids. In my experience, the majority of men who leave their children's mother have difficulty keeping ties with the children. Studies support these observations.[24]

Iris is a beautiful young woman who was married to a respectable young man. They were blessed to have to two healthy boys. Sadly, a few years after the last child was born, the marriage hit the rocks and ended in divorce. The young man went his way, and Iris was left to feed, cloth, heal, counsel and finance the entire household with no help. Iris has borne the load alone with the help of the Lord and the support network of the household of faith.

Her former husband supplied no help whatsoever. He even neglected birthdays, holidays and other special events. One would think that knowing two little boys are your own flesh and blood would be enough to make you do the right thing, but in this case it wasn't. It's no surprise that when couples stay married, the men tend to stay connected with the children as well. So if marriage is part of the solution for fatherlessness, the decline of marriage must be addressed.

Until recently, the majority of research dealing with ills in the African American family structure focused on slavery, economics and other social factors. While not denying the impact of those factors, researchers M. Belinda Tucker and Claudia Mitchell-Kernan bring other causes to the table. The three causal factors they see as contributing to the decline of African American marriages are mate availability, marital feasibility and desirability of marriage.[25]

After World War II, the "marriage squeeze" occurred. This squeeze was caused by a shortage of available mates due to the slow increase of birth rates and the fact that women generally married slightly older men. The obvious impact of the marriage squeeze was fewer marriages and an increase in unhealthy forms of relationships that produced fatherless children. On several occasions, I've had talented and capable women (young and old) come to me in frustration and say, "Pastor Mark, where are the men? It seems like the good ones are already taken and the rest are on drugs or in jail."

Tucker and Mitchell-Kernan also indicate that marital feasibility has contributed to the decline in African American marriages. The primary Achilles heel in marital feasibility is economics. We must face the facts: If a woman is courted by a man who has nothing to offer her in terms of economics, education or spiritual maturity, she is not going to want to pursue a relationship with him. She knows she can do better. So she passes the opportunity up and moves on, still choosing to be single. By the same token, a man usually doesn't want to marry a woman without being able to contribute to her economic well-being.

A few years ago, *Newsweek* published an article titled "The Black Gender Gap." It focused on the historic strides that black women were making on campuses and in the workplace. While all of this was overdue and wonderful, the flip side was these women were being forced to rethink their relationship paradigm. While they were climbing up the educational and economic ladder, a large percentage of black men were not, thus creating a gap.

This gap makes it difficult to connect and forge meaningful and lasting relationships, especially marriage. Lana Coleman, a Pasadena, California, attorney, said, "I figured that as I made more money and got the education that's required to get a job, that would make it easier for me to find someone. But it's really been the opposite." Gwen Mckinney, a married and successful Washington public-relations-firm owner made this statement: "I just consider myself like the Marines—the few, the proud—in terms of being so fortunate that I have a spouse who is supportive." She believed her husband's comfort level was due to the fact that their relationship was solid prior to the success of her business. Unfortunately, many men are threatened by successful women, thus preventing the possibility of marriage.[26]

In his book *Black Men Obsolete, Single, Dangerous?* Haki R. Madubuti taps into the frustration and pathos that many black males feel about their economic situation and how that affects their relationships with women.

> Black men in the United States are virtually powerless, landless and moneyless in a land where white manhood is measured by such acquisitions. Most African Americans have been unable to look at their lives in a historical-racial-political-economic context. Thereby, without the proper tools to analyze, many Black men have defined their lives as a duplicate of the white male ethos. The problem (and there are many) is that black men in relationship to black women cannot, a great majority of the time, deliver the "American dream." Therefore the dream is often translated into a Black male/female nightmare where Black men are acting out of frustration and ignorance, and adopt attitudes that are not productive or progressive in relationship to Black women.[27]

The words he uses—*powerless, moneyless, frustration*—are those I've heard many African American males use to express how they feel. Those deep-seated feelings and the reality of economic deprivation keep many black men from taking the hand of the one they love in marriage. They won't do it, because they don't deem it a feasible solution. They feel they can never give the woman all the things she needs or deserves. Unfortunately, other options they choose, such as cohabitation or simply having children out of wedlock, are far worse than being married and broke, because cohabitation is often short-lived and far less stable than marriage.[28]

Finally, Tucker and Mitchell-Kernan state that a decline in African American marriage is due to a lack of marriage desirability. While the desire to marry has stayed fairly intact, the "normative imperative" has changed. It's no longer normative to marry, stay married, have children and be faithful to one's spouse. Americans are open to other relationship options and have become increasingly accepting of singlehood. Most say they desire to marry but will get around to it when they get around to it.

The Pervasiveness of Divorce

While marriage is on the decline, divorce is on the rise. Sociologist Sara McLanahan writes, "Divorce rates have more than doubled in most countries between 1960 and 1990; in some countries they increased fourfold."[29] Divorce is probably one of the most vicious causes of father absenteeism; everybody loses, especially the children. Gallagher makes this observation:

> Few people realize how difficult it is to transplant the relationships of family life to the impoverished ground of the visiting relationship. One of the sad and surprising truths we are beginning to face is that unmarriage radically alters the father-child relationship. The children almost always experience this transformation as a profound loss.[30]

When Dad leaves, he may tell his son, "Daddy and Mommy can't live together, but I will always be there for you, son." The stark reality is, he won't be there, or he will be there in a way that is drastically different from what the child needs. When the father leaves, his finances usually leave. The day-to-day interaction with his child and the emotional contribution leave as well. If the dad happens to marry and adopts a new family, the child may be seen as a drain on the financial resources the father needs to support his new family. It's a chilling, cold reality. Popenoe confirms it:

> But the larger truth is that most divorced fathers in America, for whatever reason, lose almost all contact with their children over time. They withdraw from their children's lives. They become terrible fathers. And for those noncustodial men who maintain some contact, the reality that a co-residence between a father and son is necessary, is not always a sufficient basis for sound and effective fatherhood.[31]

A close friend and fellow pastor recently attended the funeral of a man in his early forties. The deceased was the former husband of a woman who attends his church and the father of her two sons. Several years before, the man had run off with another woman and divorced his wife. After he remarried, he totally neglected his boys. He went on to become a prosperous businessman, but gave his children from the previous marriage nothing. All his money, time and emotion were invested in his new family. Adding to this tragedy was that the man's two sons by his first wife were not even acknowledged at the funeral. So my friend was left to minister to two teenage boys who were fatherless while their dad was alive and not even acknowledged at his death.

Our culture embraces divorce. It's almost easier to get out of a marriage than it is to enter into one. Television and radio are flooded with advertisements from divorce attorneys who promise to help you attain your just reward from a settlement. Laws have been changed to make it easier for people to divorce for any reason. Books line the shelves on how a person can have a healthy divorce. Celebrities are hailed for divorcing a spouse who was not growing as fast in his or her career. As a pastor I have counseled with individuals forty and under who are on their second or third try at marriage. Yet divorce is responsible for millions of fatherless children in our nation. Some of the effects of divorce on children will be discussed in the next chapter.

The Increase of Single Motherhood

Our church, Life Change Christian Center, is located in the city of Portland, Oregon. In Portland alone, there are 26,394 single-parent homes. The majority of those twenty-six-thousand-plus homes are cared for by women. Men account for 6,531 of the single-parent homes, while women lead the other 19,836.[32] This implies that the majority of children in our ministry area do not have fathers. In fact, in Portland, Big Brothers Big Sisters has over two thousand kids on their waiting list waiting to be paired with mentors. From my conversation with an employee of the organization, almost 70 percent of these children come from single-parent homes, in most of which the mom is the present parent.

And ours is not an isolated situation. On a national level, Wade Horn and Tom Sylvester write, "Of women entering their childbearing years, half will experience female headship at some point in their childbearing years, compared to the one-third a generation ago. Nearly 80% of all Black women will be the head of their families at some point in their childbearing years."[33] The Urban League's 1990 report on the state of black America says that single mothers made up 60 percent of African American family structures.[34]

In every type of negative statistic concerning family issues, African Americans appear to be at the top of the chart. This doesn't mean that all familial and social diseases are perpetrated by single mothers. In the words of Stokely Carmichael, "The reason we are in the bag we are in is not because of Mama, it's because of what they did to Mama."[35] What did they do to Mama? A brief inquiry into the institution of slavery may provide a few answers.

For two centuries, the iron jaw of slavery ravaged the black family with implications that are still felt today. In his book *Urban Ministry*, David Claerbaut writes, "To understand Black American life necessitates sensitivity to these eras, for the present social and economic condition of black America is largely the outgrowth of slavery and segregation."[36] One of the by-products of slavery is the single mother and the absent father. Slavery forced the matriarch to be the backbone of the family while the black man struggled to exist.

Slave owners who used the law for their own greed deliberately crafted this scenario. Tucker and Mitchell-Kernan say, "Colonial slave masters quickly established the right to define and structure the most intimate connections and activities of their slaves and servants, electing to control various aspects of their sexual behavior and family life through power as lawmakers."[37]

During this period, the courts were even convinced that the slave owner was given a divine order to be the moral guardian over the slave family. Hence, slaves had no legal authority over their children, and children were named after their owner, not their parents. This meant the ultimate allegiance was to the master rather than to the parents.[38]

In 1662 an act was passed that forced black children, regardless of the color or condition of their father, to take on the status of their mother. The implications of this law impacted the black family for centuries. First, it provided a legal context for matrifocal kinship groups to exist throughout slavery. Second, it allowed slave owners to identify the child with the mother and in many cases to ignore the role of the father totally on all levels.[39]

Lorenzo Ivy, a former slave, tells about a typical scenario that often happened to families during slavery:

My master was very good to his slaves, and they thought a great deal of him. But all our happy days were over when he went south and caught the cotton fever. . . . He tuk two of my aunts an' lef der husbands up heah an' he separated all tergther seven husbands an' wives. One 'oman had twelve chillin. Yessuh! Separated dem all an' tuk 'em south wif him to Gregory and Alabamy.[40]

The family unit was broken up by the slave owner, which left the wife "widowed" and at the helm of the family, with the father far away. Patterns etched over two centuries are hard to break. When you add in other factors such as economics, education, socialization, racism and sin, the cycle is even more difficult to break. However, the future need not be like the past; the cycle must be broken. Black mothers need to be united with the fathers of their children so that fatherless children can experience the blessing of a dad.

Work

Work can be another cause of father absenteeism. Lee Beaty cites career demands as a major cause of father absenteeism.[41] One of the traits that marks our society is long hours in the office. Many fathers simply don't take the time to consider that every decision they make to spend long hours at the job is a decision to spend long hours away from their children.

Harry Chapin's classic song "Cats in the Cradle" captures the essence of this problem. In the song, a little boy, longing to spend time with his father, asks, "When are ya comin' home, Dad?" To which the dad replies, "Don't know when, but we will have a good time then, son." In many cases, as in this song, the "then" comes too late. Psychologist Donald Swan states that work-related absences "from a child's perspective creates a father who is home for sleep and food and is otherwise withdrawn and preoccupied."[42]

Long hours are not the only problem when it comes to work; no hours are problematic as well. When a father can't find work, sometimes he's forced to make decisions to find employment that separates him from his family. One of the things I like to do is talk to cashiers about the Lord. So much of my time is occupied by "churchy stuff" that I like to use my times at the store or the gas station to witness for Jesus. On one occasion, while I was waiting for my gas to finish pumping, I was talking to the clerk to see if he knew the Lord or went to church. He replied that he was holding down a couple of jobs, so he couldn't fit church in.

I asked him about his family, and the floodgates opened. He said he couldn't find a job back home, so he had moved to Oregon and had been separated from his family for over a year. He went on to explain how he and his wife were not on good terms and that he missed his kids. Of course, there may be more to the story. But the reason this cashier gave me for being separated from his kids for a whole year was his inability to find work.

The Father's Relationship with the Child's Mother

The status of the relationship between a father and his child's mother can greatly affect the involvement a father has in the life of his child. Jennifer Hamer, a professor of African American studies, discovered that three types of relationships exist between mothers and nonresident fathers: friendly relationships, intimate relationships and antagonistic relationships.[43] A friendly relationship encourages a father to maintain contact with his children. It allows the father to stay in contact by phone. He is free to ask the mother about the child's daily activities, and the mother is free to express to the father the child's daily needs.

The intimate relationship consists of a sexual relationship between the father and mother. This, however, doesn't mean the mother and father are monogamous or even intend to get married. The fathers in this situation feel they have a good relationship with their children. The difference between the intimate and the friendly relationship is that the father in the intimate relationship feels obligated not only to the child, but to the mother as well. When present, the father is actively involved in all aspects of the child's life. However, this relationship can be volatile, and when it becomes strained, so does the father's relationship with his child.

The last relationship is the antagonistic relationship. It can be characterized by the Hatfield and McCoy family feud. It inhibits and discourages the father's involvement in the child's life. The father may see the mother as a gold digger who is out to take him down, as a bad mother or as an enemy who is trying to hurt him through the child. In this relationship, phone calls are denied, visitation rights are refused and in some cases the mother and child move without telling the father.

Recently in our church, Greg—who had freshly come to faith in Christ—approached me with a prayer request. I could see from the look on his face that he was deeply troubled and needed some comfort. He said to me, "Pastor, pray for me. I feel I need to re-connect with my son, but I can't because his mother is *trippin'*." In other words, the antagonistic relationship between him and the child's mother was hampering his involvement in the child's life. In times past, he had felt it wasn't worth the fight, the mind games and the emotional gymnastics, so he basically had given up trying to connect with his child.

This scenario is not unusual. Many fathers are estranged from their children because someone is "trippin'." Sadly, some fathers give up the battle too soon. The good news about Greg's story is that the Spirit of God had awakened within him his paternal responsibility, and he was working to reconnect with his child. Should his effort prove to be successful, his child will know that he has a father who loves him and values him.

The conclusion of Hamer's study speaks of the mother as the gatekeeper, inhibiting or encouraging the role of the father in the child's experience. The blows of a broken relationship can make it hard for a mother or father to keep the door open. Unfortunately, many mothers have made the decision to keep it shut and thereby keep the child from his or her father.

Teen Pregnancy

Teen pregnancy is problematic from a number of standpoints. First, when a teenage girl becomes pregnant, generally she lacks the economic and sometimes the relational structure to support herself and the child adequately. In the 1940s and '50s, the majority of pregnant teens got married to the father of the child. This is not the case today. If the mother decides to keep the child, she's generally left with all the weight of rearing the child while the father exits the picture. Tragically, our culture often strokes him for placing another notch on his belt.

Nine out of ten African American teen mothers are single, and the numbers seem to be growing.[44] Sadly, besides the possibility of being one of the 9.3 million children who have no legally identified father, children of teen mothers have a greater chance of being incarcerated later in life, thus perpetuating the cycle of fatherless children.[45]

Alice is a young woman I've known since she was learning to walk. When she was in her mid-teens, she became pregnant and had a child. Alice had been a young woman with a bright future before her, but suddenly she was not only faced with finishing high school, growing and maturing, but also with raising a child. One day I was driving down the street and saw her, so I rolled down my window and asked, "Hey, Alice, when are you coming to church?"

She replied, "I'm so mad I can't pass the job skill requirement test. I've tried several times, and I can't do it."

I could hear the frustration in her voice, and her body language confirmed her disappointment as well. For her, passing the test was not just to help her feel better about herself; it would also make it possible for her to take care of her child. Failing the test meant less money. Less money meant less money for food, less money for rent and less money to take care of her and her baby's needs. What an incredible burden for a teenage girl!

I tried to encourage her to keep trying, and I told her I would pray for her as she asked. When I rolled up the window, my heart was heavy because I knew her background and I knew this teenage girl bore the burden of succeeding not only for herself, but also for her little one.

Incarceration

One day I was waiting to have my glasses adjusted and ran into the mother of a young girl who attends our church infrequently. I made some small talk with the mom and told her it was good to have Sue attending our church. Her response was, "You need to really talk to her, because last night she lost her mind." The mom went on to tell me that her daughter couldn't get over the fact that her father was in jail and wouldn't be getting out for a long time.

Incarceration definitely contributes to father absenteeism, especially for black males and children. Dorothy Roberts writes, "Blacks, mostly men, make up over half of the one million inmates in American jails. The racial disparity in incarceration rates continues to rise, with nearly eight Blacks in state and federal prisons in 1994 for each White person incarcerated."[46]

Statistics from the Bureau of Justice also shed light on the problem of incarceration for African American males:

- There are 34 sentenced African American male inmates per 1,000 African American men in the United States, versus only 4 sentenced white male inmates per 1,000 white men.
- Over the course of a lifetime, 28% of African American men will enter a state or federal prison.[47]

Being incarcerated makes it difficult, if not impossible, to be a father. Even when the father is released from prison, he faces daunting odds. The difficulty of finding employment once discharged and the reintegration process into society provide unique challenges to being an available and good father.

We've looked at many factors that have created the fatherlessness problem we're addressing in this book. Now it's time to examine the impact that father absenteeism has on children.

2

THE IMPACT OF FATHERLESSNESS

Jeremiah the prophet proclaimed, "In those days people will no longer say, 'The fathers have eaten sour grapes, and the children's teeth are set on edge.' Instead, everyone will die for his own sin; whoever eats sour grapes—his own teeth will be set on edge" (Jer 31:29-30). His purpose in articulating this widespread belief was to stress that each person is responsible for his or her own sins. While the prophetic injunction places the moral responsibility on each individual, there is still some truth in the "sour grapes" saying. A father's actions impact the lives of his children. The teeth of our nation's children are being set on edge by the sour grapes of father absenteeism.

While it's true that not all children are affected in tragic ways, all miss out on needed blessing when a father isn't present. Many people who have grown up without fathers have done very well psychologically, socially and economically. In fact, Leighton Ford in *Transforming Leadership* mentions a study by Dr. Pierre Rentchnick that found that many of the world's greatest leaders were orphans or had simply been abandoned by their parents. Some of the names he listed were George Washington, Golda Meir and Alexander the Great.[1]

Personally, I also know some healthy people who have grown up without a father present. So the impact of father absenteeism on the lives of people is by no means deterministic. However, children face several identifiable problems and risks when abandoned by their fathers, and they must grapple with these problems to lead a healthy life. In the following pages, we'll examine the impact of father absenteeism in different areas of a person's life.

Pain

Charnetta Hutson is a young woman who grew up coping with the issues of an absent father. She wrote a song called "Daddy's Girl" that deals with the pain of a father absence. Consider her words:

> I'm a fatherless child, it's all I ever been
> It's all I ever be, since you're gone from me
> Still I hope you know, that I can never unlove you, love you
> 1974 was a year things changed
> Too much alcohol makes people violent and strange
> You broke the windows with a baseball bat
> As my mother cried inside with me on her lap
> The dream destroyed, it was time to leave
> She didn't take much, just a few things of lovin me
> That was the birth of this fatherless child
> And a struggling mother with the world in her eyes
> She did it though, put herself in college
> Raisin me wit grace, givin me the knowledge
> And Pops you, you never came by
> Never sent money never called to say hi
>
> I use to lie to the other kids on the block
> Say I knew where you was at so the questions would stop

I fronted to my friends that you didn't mean much
But I use to cry alone, and long for your touch
Would I be easier to love, not so torn inside
If you would've beat that man, and stood by my side?
Would I write sad songs, and call pain daily?
How different would I be if you had raised me?[2]

One injury that father absenteeism inflicts on many lives is pain. Charnetta's song gives an insightful view into the pain she experienced through her formative years. The causes of Charnetta's pain are obvious: the rejection, abandonment, disappointment, emptiness and, finally, hopelessness. She concludes her father is gone, but she hopes he knows she loves him.

In *Whatever Happened to Daddy's Little Girl?* Barras tells of her pain in not having a father present.

I know fatherlessness. I know the emptiness it creates, the years searching for something to fill the void, looking for a substitute to make me whole. I know the insecurity; the endless battles that are recreated with each new relationship—battles that are never won; the pain that resurfaces after the departure of each man in my life. I wanted women to understand the distinct patterns of sadness, insecurity, confusion and unresolved pain that connects those of us who experience a father's loss either through death, divorce, or abandonment.[3]

Notice the distinct similarities between Mystic's and Barras's pain: the void, the insecurities and the hopelessness. Though these two women probably have never met, probably were born in different environments and are at different ages, father absenteeism unites them in a song of pain.

The pain caused by father absence is not isolated to women and girls; boys and men are equally affected. Several times during services, at prayer meetings in our church and in one-on-one conversations, I have had boys and men break down and cry because they had no father in their lives.

I remember a conversation I had with Hank, a man in his early twenties. Our conversation turned to his upbringing, and when he began to talk about his father, he fell on the floor and began to sob like a baby. Hank's father had abandoned him and his family when he was a very young child, and the emotions and the issues of not having his father around seemed to come tumbling down on him during our conversation.

Donald Swan writes about the emotional impact a father's absence can have on boys prior to age six:

> According to Johnson (1993) emotional correlates of father absence are more prominent when the absence occurred prior to age 6. Examples include intense anger and lower self-control. Childhood psychopathology included nightmares, bed-wetting, withdrawal, fears and somatic complaints. Emotional symptoms were found to be markedly more severe in boys than in girls.[4]

All the symptoms Swan mentioned point to one thing: the child's pain. However, the pain that a boy experiences in childhood doesn't stay localized there. In many instances the pain is carried into his teen years and into adulthood.[5]

One primary reason for the pain caused by father absenteeism is "father hunger." Robert McGee, the founder of Rapha, a nationally recognized health care organization that provides care for people suffering from psychiatric and substance abuse problems, defines father hunger as emptiness, an unfulfilled desire, a gnawing deep within one's spirit and a continual craving to experience love from one's father.[6] Maggie Gallagher speaks of father hunger in this fashion:

> It's an ache in the heart, a gnawing anxiety in the gut. It's a longing for a man, not just for a woman, who will care for

you, protect you, and show you how to survive in the world. For a boy especially, it's the raw, persistent, desperate hunger for dependable male love, and an image of maleness that is not at odds with love: Father hunger.[7]

This hunger affects individuals in the deepest levels of their being. It's like physical hunger—when food isn't available for long periods, pain and anguish set in. When an individual longs for the love of a father and the father isn't present to meet the need, emotional, psychological and social hunger pains can and do strike, leaving the child or adult to wrestle with the pain. Today many people are feeling the hunger pains and are trying desperately to stop the growling.

Poverty

A friend of mine, Curtis Kimbrough, wrote his life story in a book titled *How I Got Over!* In the opening pages, he gives a snapshot of his childhood. Aspects of his story are key in the discussion of the impact of father absenteeism as it relates to poverty. Curtis was born in Indianapolis, where he lived with his mother and siblings in what he describes as an ugly, concrete, three-story building called "The Projects." His family shared the second floor with five other families, which were mostly poor or lower middle class.

While Curtis says that he has some fond memories of Lockfield Gardens, he can still remember families arguing and fighting, and teenagers hanging out in the hallways, sniffing glue from paper bags. Since he was the second youngest, he looked to his older siblings for protection and guidance, even though they also were children.

When Curtis was about two, his father, Buck, left home. Buck had a bad drinking problem, and Curtis's mother refused to put up with it, so out he went. A few years later, the couple tried to reconcile, but the attempt lasted only for a couple of days. (Buck died in his forties from the effects of alcoholism.)

Curtis's mother worked hard to support the family, working

long hours. Frequently she worked nights, which meant the kids had to take care of themselves during the day. To provide clothing for the family, she frequented a Goodwill store. Curtis went on to say that, during those days, they ate a lot of cornbread, beans and mayonnaise sandwiches. He also added that though they were poor, the suffering was minimized by his mother's and others' efforts.[8]

Curtis's story communicates a reality that exists in the lives of many fatherless children. That reality is poverty. Statistics show that single female-headed homes are at a greater risk of poverty than the rest of the general population. The report "America's Children: Key National Indicators of Well-Being 2001" states, "Children in father absent homes are five times more likely to be poor. In 1999, 8 percent of children of married couples were living in poverty, compared to the 42 percent of children in female-householder families."[9] Compounding the issue is the fact that single mothers are not only more prone to experience poverty, but the severity of their poverty is greater. Also, single mothers are more likely to experience persistent poverty.

Studies show that after a divorce, a woman and her children's income drops about 40 percent. Their living standards fall about two-thirds below their previous levels. On the other hand, the man's income dips only 15 percent, and he is slightly better off the year following the divorce than he was the previous year.[10]

As in the case of Curtis's family, divorce usually places a greater economic strain on the mother than on the father. The mother is generally left with the children, and her earning power and opportunities are generally slimmer than they are for men. So the divorced woman is hit with a double dilemma. First, she has to raise the children on substantially less income than what she had when a husband was present. Second, she loses half of her support network and has to find other avenues to care for the children adequately while she works a job that usually inadequately supports her household.

Hence, the child support wars rage. In my ministry I've had numerous conversations with struggling mothers who are trying to get the dad to pay at least a portion of his child support. Some of the things that men do to avoid paying child support are quite disturbing. According to the U.S. Census Bureau, "In 2007, the proportion of child support received by mothers (62.5 percent) and fathers (63.8 percent). Custodial mothers were given $18.6 billion of the $29.8 billion in support that was due, and custodial fathers received $2.8 billion of the $4.3 billion that was due."[11] Other studies show that fathers are generally obligated to pay 17 percent of their income for one child and 25 percent for two. In 1991, 11.9 billion dollars were paid, while 17.7 billion remained uncollected. If court orders matched fathers' ability to pay, the amount owed would be close to 50 billion.[12] Deadbeat dads are difficult to resuscitate, and children are suffering while mothers and those who enforce legislation struggle to make these fathers provide monetary resources for their offspring.

Poverty is an evil in the lives of children because of the positive things it excludes them from. In many cases, poverty forbids children from growing up in a healthy environment with decent housing. Curtis's story illustrates the inability of an impoverished mother and children to have a place to live in a safe and healthy environment. A family with means is not going to live in a complex where families constantly fight, kids openly do drugs in the hallways and violence is commonplace outside the front door. Most of us would start trying to get our family out of that environment the very day we entered it. The child in poverty is not afforded that option, nor is his mother. They simply have to stick it out and make the best of a situation in which the odds are greatly stacked against them.

In many instances, poverty also forbids them good health care. Researcher L. V. Klerman listed several conditions that are found more often in children who were a part of a household whose income was less than 10,000 dollars annually. In children of families whose income was 35,000 dollars annually, these health issues were less frequent. Klerman found that children who are poor are more likely to experience the following:

- Infectious diseases, such as rheumatic fever, hemophilus influenza, meningitis, gastroenteritis and parasitic diseases. Other diseases for which there are vaccines are also more widespread, due to a lower immunization rate. Also AIDS is found more often in poor children because of the mother's drug use.

- Vision and hearing problems are found more often in poor children, as well as dental problems.

- Psychosocial and psychosomatic problems are greater in poor children. Studies show that there is a link between income and some of the emotional and behavioral problems.

- Lead poisoning is also problematic. Inner-city, underprivileged kids have the highest levels of PbB in their blood.

- Poor children have the greatest rate of intentional injuries. Families with incomes under 15,000 dollars experience a higher rate of physical, sexual and emotional abuse. Also they experience a greater degree of emotional and educational neglect.[13]

The problem of poverty is that it not only makes a child more vulnerable to a plethora of illnesses, it also limits her or his ability to break out of the vicious cycle. Children of poverty have fewer opportunities, and many lack the necessary support to succeed in a world where dollars and cents can affect their health, welfare and destiny.

Teen Pregnancy
Her name is Lisa, and she's a gifted young woman with much promise. Lisa's father abandoned her for the streets and all the ad-

diction trappings that accompany such a lifestyle. On several occasions throughout her teenage years, attempts at reconciliation were made. These futile attempts only produced within her greater pain, frustration and disappointment because her father failed to uphold his end of the contract. He continuously broke promises, and out the door he went again and again.

Not understanding her real need, Lisa began to medicate her pain through illicit relationships. What she discovered was that after the young men satisfied their wants, they left her as well. This created a greater crisis, for she reasoned that if her dad abandoned her and her so-called boyfriends all left, men couldn't be trusted. Compounding these issues is the fact that she is pregnant with a baby girl.

What Lisa lacked was genuine unconditional love from a good male role model. The result was twofold. First, she thought an immoral relationship would satisfy her need for love. Second, her trust level as it relates to men was destroyed. These two elements alone usually lead to teen pregnancy and single motherhood.

Lisa's tendency to blur the lines between genuine love and sex is not uncommon among teenage girls who grow up with no father in the home. In their study on the effects of father absenteeism on female development and college attendance, Franklin Krohn and Zoe Bogan write, "Adolescent girls raised in fatherless households are far more likely to engage in promiscuous sexual activity before marriage, to cohabit, to get pregnant out of wedlock and to have an abortion."[14] McLanahan states that the teen birth risk for girls in average two-parent, white families with some college education is 8 percent, while the risk for average one-parent, white homes is 22 percent. In black homes, the average risk is 26 percent for two-parent households and 40 percent for one-parent families.

According to McLanahan, risk factors increase for girls whose parents are disadvantaged, meaning the parents have less than a high school education. The risk factors for teen pregnancy among this demographic for whites are 19 percent for two-parent and 44 percent for one-parent households. For blacks, there is a 29 percent teen-pregnancy risk for two-parent and 45 percent for one-parent households. For Hispanics, it is a 24 percent risk of teen pregnancy for two-parent homes and a 46 percent risk for one-parent homes.[15]

Lisa's distrust of men also produces an obstacle. Without trust, there can be no lasting relationships, let alone a long-term marriage. Studies show that girls who have little contact with their fathers, especially during adolescence, have great difficulties forming lasting relationships with men. In some cases, they shy away from males altogether, or they become sexually aggressive. Krohn and Bogan say that girls with involved fathers learn how to act in relationships with males because they use the father-daughter relationship as a model.[16] In our community, we don't see a pattern of shying away from men; in many cases, aggression is displayed. Often I see a young woman having multiple children by different men. Commitment is not even a consideration. Hence the cycle is perpetuated.

Crime and Violence

CBS aired a *60 Minutes* interview with a young man in prison named Sanyika Shakur, a.k.a. Kody Scott, "The Monster." Shakur was a notorious gang leader in South Central Los Angeles. At the time of the interview, he was twenty-nine years old. For at least sixteen of his twenty-nine years, he had been involved in crime and violence. He earned the name "The Monster" at age thirteen, when he stomped a robbery victim for twenty minutes, leaving him in a coma and permanently disfigured. His life of crime consisted of robberies, murders and a long list of other offenses.

During the interview, Steve Kroft questioned Shakur about his reason for living a life of delinquency and violence. Kroft said to him, "You don't have the typical excuses or reasons: you didn't grow up in the projects, you had a very strong mother and your father is . . . "

Shakur abruptly replied, "Absent! Missing in action."

Shakur's biological father was a professional football player. His father's fame meant nothing to Shakur because, he went on to say, "While my father was on the football field, I was on the streets and he never came." At this point, Shakur, with his hands chained, placed his head down and began to rub his face on his shirt to wipe away his tears.[17] This is the only time Shakur showed any type of remorse or sorrow in the interview, even when asked about the number of people he had killed and other gruesome details. Only when asked about his father did he cry and forsake his "cool" demeanor.

To say that the absence of Shakur's father was the total driving force behind his life of crime and violence is likely too simplistic. On the other hand, it can't be denied that the absence of his father factored into the equation.

Over the last several decades, social scientists have indicated a link between adolescent crime and father absence. Elaine Rodney and Robert Mupier state that violent children are eleven times more likely not to live with fathers and six times more likely to have unmarried parents. In many cases, they assumed that children who are in this category are being raised in non-nurturing environments and lack the blessing of an effective masculine role model.[18]

In the same fashion, African American boys who live in father-absent homes or who are in situations with poor parent relationships were found to exhibit low self-esteem and hypermasculinity.[19] A father's presence helps to curb criminal behavior.[20]

David Popenoe makes several observations linking the rise of juvenile crime to fatherlessness. He states that since 1960 the crime rate in America has soared by 550 percent, with youth making the greatest statistical contribution. Referring to data from the National Father Initiative, Popenoe states that in "America, 60 percent of all rapists, 72 percent of adolescent murders, and 70 percent of long-term prison inmates come from fatherless homes."[21]

As a pastor, I've had to deal with a number of young men who have committed serious crimes, ranging from petty thefts to murder. In most of these cases, the young men have no or very limited father involvement in their lives. In his article "All My Friends are Dying," Larry Elder contends that one of the primary reasons for crime, especially among young blacks, is absentee fathers: "Absentee, noninvolved fathers are the primary reason behind the Department of Justice statistics showing that 32 percent of young blacks possess criminal records versus the seven percent of their white counterparts."[22]

In our church, the reality of this statistic hits home. A large portion of families either have a male family member in jail or have had a male family member there. I'm disturbed because of the possibility of future implications. Currently, 58.6 percent of all African American children live in single-parent homes. Almost 90 percent of those homes are female-headed.[23] This creates a greater vulnerability to poverty and its ill effects on the children. If past performance is indicative of future behavior, the years to come will produce a great deal of crime among our youth.

When a father is present in the home, he has the opportunity to help shape and develop his child's life in an up-close and personal way. He can be a good role model for his child. He can teach his child empathy, respect and wholesome social values. When the father is absent, this natural platform for training is missing.

Researcher Lee Beaty discusses the effects of paternal absence on male adolescents and peer relationships. He states that the greatest negative impact occurs if the father leaves before the child turns five and the greatest impact is on boys. He writes that when these children grow older, they tend to be more dependent on their peers and more ambiguous about masculinity, to disfavor competitive games and sports, and to engage in more aggressive behavior toward females. Boys whose fathers are absent are prone to take less satisfactory behavioral paths.[24]

In the same study, Beaty cites a study by Michael Lamb that demonstrates how paternal absences affect relationships among adolescent boys. He stresses that peers supply a strong role model for boys. This is a crucial insight, because if a young person's peer network espouses a criminal and violent element, that youth is going to be influenced to engage in antisocial behavior. However, if the father is present, he may be able to influence the child positively and thus slow down the rise in juvenile crime and violence. The ancient sage wrote,

> My son, if sinners entice you, do not give in to them. If they say, "Come along with us; let's lie in wait for someone's blood, let's waylay some harmless soul; let's swallow them alive, like the grave, and whole, like those who go down to the pit; we will get all sorts of valuable things and fill our houses with plunder; throw in your lot with us, and we will share a common purse"—my son, do not go along with them, do not set foot on their paths; for their feet rush into sin, they are swift to shed blood. How useless to spread a net in full view of all the birds! These men lie in wait for their own blood; they waylay only themselves! Such is the end of all who go after ill-gotten gain; it takes away the lives of those who get it. (Prov 1:10-19)

In my community, we have too many young men losing their lives for ill-gotten gain. We need fathers to take them as little boys and not simply tell them to stop, but model and show them how to not ever get involved in crime.

Education

A popular minister told the story of his first days in school. When he was a little boy, he was chubby and had limited physical abilities. His lack of prowess created a problem because to get to school each day, he had to climb over a large rock. For the other kids, it was the highlight of the morning trek to school, but for him it presented a monumental challenge. The Everest-size rock brought him to tears every day. One day the boy's father grabbed a few tools, went to the trail and began to level the rock. When he was finished, the rock was gone, and so was the obstacle that stood in the way of the journey to school.

Children face many obstacles in the educational process, but when a father is present, he can help to level some of the hard places along the path. Children in one-parent households statistically have lower grade-point averages and less desire to go to college. In addition, children of two-parent households are more likely to stay in school. For single-parent homes, the high school dropout rate is 29 percent compared to 13 percent in two-parent families.[25] Also, children living apart from their biological parents are four times more likely to be suspended or expelled from school than children living with both parents.[26] A child can't excel in school if he or she isn't in school, and fathers along with mothers are an integral part of helping a child stay in school.

A father is also essential to a child's education because he can minimize distractions. The gnawing distraction of the pain of not having Dad around can move a child's concentration from the classroom to trying to solve adult problems in an adult world—problems she or he has no power to change. This creates emotional distress that is hard enough for adults to work through, let alone children. If the father is present and involved in the child's life, that particular emotional dissonance is absent, which allows the child to function more effectively in school.

A father's financial contribution also plays a role in his children's education. In her paper "Life Without Father: What Happens to Children?" McLanahan states that in 1995 the U.S. Census reported that the median income level for two-parent homes was fifty thousand dollars, while the median for single-mother households—which make up more than half of those living in poverty—was under eighteen thousand.[27] The income level of the parent affects where a child attends school. The poorer a child, the poorer the quality of education he or she receives. The better schools are generally located in more economically affluent neighborhoods. You hardly ever hear of parents intentionally sending their children to an inner-city school to enable them to get a good education. The absence of a father diminishes the family's income, which in turn increases the risk of a negative educational experience for the child.

In a study on the effects of father absenteeism on female college students, Krohn and Bogan show that women who grow up without a father often forgo college for a paycheck.[28] The women have watched their mothers struggle for years and beg for money in court for child support, and so they vow they will never allow themselves to be placed in that position. Getting a job and a paycheck represents freedom for them. As a result, they reduce their value in the marketplace and in many cases end up with jobs that don't pay very well.

Finally, fathers can help with behavioral problems. The 1989 film *Lean on Me* told the true story of Joe Clark, a man who transformed a delinquent high school into a place of learning and education. The first tall order Clark faced was to bring discipline to the school; the teachers couldn't teach, because the kids were out of control. Once the kids calmed down and learned to behave correctly, the teachers were able to teach them.

As Zimmerman, Salem and Notaro state, fathers play a key role in reducing problematic behaviors in their children, especially boys.[29] When the father is absent, the child is more apt to be in the principal's office, skipping school, in fights and in trouble with the law. If a father is present, he can help direct the child in the correct way.

Mother-Child Relationship

If a father is absent, the relationship a child has with her or his mother can be affected. McLanahan states,

> The economic hardship and insecurity of single motherhood can bring on depression and psychological distress, thereby interfering with good motherhood. Even among middle-class families, the departure of the father can trigger disruptions in the household routines such as meals and bedtime, and undermine discipline. With their time, energy, and spirit stretched thin, some single mothers become too lenient and others become too rigid or strict. Neither mothering style bodes well for children.[30]

A person only has so much to give before he or she is stretched too thin. Curtis's mom wasn't home much of the time because she had to work. Though she did a great job with her kids, there were things she wanted to do and times she wanted to be with them but couldn't, because of other demands. Just recently, I was involved in a situation where a couple of young girls got into a squabble with a local convenience store owner. We ended up having to call the girls' mother. The mom left her job and came to the store to straighten out the situation. When we were leaving the store, the mom wasn't only troubled by the incident, but also expressed with great disappointment to her young daughter that this incident cost her a specific amount of money.

That type of pressure can and does affect a mother's relationship with her children. When a father is present, he can help buffer some of the stressful aspects of parenting, thus giving the mom a much-needed break to recoup and interact with the kids in a more refreshed and less stressed fashion.

Father absenteeism is a dagger inflicting injury on our children. Other factors such as the environment, culture, poverty and education do play a role in the problems I've discussed. However, the absence of fathers makes a massive contribution to the social and psychological mayhem that's impacting our children. Now that we're aware of the impact of father absenteeism on the life of children, we're prepared to consider what to do about it.

PART TWO

How We Can
Help the Fatherless

3

EMBEDDING A CORPORATE FATHERLESS VALUE

When I was growing up, the favorite blanket of all us Strong kids was the tattered, battle-worn, purple blanket with a big letter L smack dab in the middle. The poor blanket endured much abuse from the hands of the five of us children, who always preferred it to the new and better blankets in the house. On many occasions, somewhat of a corporate compromise was reached. All of us would manage to place a foot or a hand or maybe even an entire leg under the blanket to enjoy the Friday-night movie along with a big bag of greasy homemade popcorn.

The attraction we all had toward this blanket was not the "Big letter L" or the radiance of the bright purple. Its specialness was embedded into our little hearts by virtue of who owned the blanket—our dad. It was his blanket from his college days. The blanket reminded us of the times we spent at our dad's knee, listening to all his stories about his childhood days and his exploits in college and the Marines.

When Dad was away on business trips, that blanket would

make all of us Strong kids feel good. Of course, as a little tyke, I had no way of articulating why the blanket gave us such a good feeling. I now know that while we were under that blanket, it brought about not just a physical warmth, but also emotional and psychological comfort that gave us a sense of security and well-being in our dad's absence.

How can our church, ministry or organization weave a blanket that gives warmth to the fatherless? How can we embed a value within our ministry culture to meet their need?

Reality checkpoint! I understand that the last thing a pastor or leader needs is the pressure or burden of creating another ministry, organization, committee or job description. Most of us are already overworked and have mounds of other responsibilities oozing over the edges of our plate. The thought of one more scoop of anything might make you say, "It's time for a diet or fast from work."

The key to embedding a corporate value in your church, organization or ministry to meet the needs of the fatherless is not creating something brand new. It's the deliberate embedding of care for the fatherless into your existing ministries, services and culture.

Just as no two people are the same, no two churches, ministries or organizations are twins either. Churches and ministries differ in size, location, demographics, emphasis and resources. Regardless of the composition of your church, ministry or organization, you already have the components in place; you simply need to embed the value.

The Biblical Perspective

From a purely compassionate human point of view, care for the fatherless is a worthy value to embrace. For the church, however, that is not our launching point. From a biblical perspective, we understand from God's point of view that care for the fatherless is not only a compassion issue, but primarily a justice one.

In Old Testament times, *justice* primarily referred to acceptable and adequate behavior, which was metered by God's standards as revealed through the Law and the Prophets.[1] When the people of God upheld these standards in the various facets of their life and conduct, justice was upheld. Failure to uphold the divine stipulations perpetrated injustices and caused harm and pain to the wronged parties and the community as a whole.

God places extreme importance and emphasis on justice to the fatherless (Ps 10:17-18; 68:5-6). Deuteronomy 10:18 reads, "He defends the cause of the fatherless and the widow, and loves the alien, giving him food and clothing." God's revelation of himself as a God of justice with particular concern for the fatherless and socially less fortunate was not simply given to Israel for information. It was given to them to imitate. Taylor indicates that there are more than forty Old Testament Scriptures that make ministry to the fatherless an act of true justice for Israel.[2]

As the Israelite community made sure it was merciful to the fatherless by providing food and shelter and by representing them in court and on the major issues affecting their lives, the paternal justice of God was satisfied. One powerful story of providing justice for the fatherless is in the biblical book that bears a parentless child's name, Esther. As a young woman, Esther was orphaned. Instead of being forced to live in an unloving and non-nurturing environment, she was taken in and raised by her cousin Mordecai, who footed the bill for her care. He provided advocacy, empowerment and mercy. Esther's needs were met; she didn't face abandonment, isolation or need. The beauty of this story lies in the fact that the orphaned child for whom Mordecai made sacrifices became God's instrument of deliverance for the entire Jewish nation.

The New Testament also illustrates the value God places on caring for the fatherless. The community of faith was to play an important role in fathering the fatherless. As in the Old Testament, where provision for the fatherless was woven into the context of the law, God placed responsibility on the New Testament community. Again, James articulated the expectation clearly: "Religion that God our Father accepts as pure and faultless is this: to look after orphans and widows in their distress and to keep oneself from being polluted by the world" (Jas 1:27).

One aspect of the community's proof of religion, or its relationship with God, is its response to orphans. Note that in first-century Palestine a child was considered an orphan if he or she had only a mother. It isn't enough to be sentimentally sorry; action is required to help alleviate some of the suffering an orphan experiences due to the absence of parents. This care of the orphans is an expectation and responsibility assigned to the community of faith.

This is just an overview of the teaching of Scripture on fatherlessness. There is much more to be drawn out. (See appendix B for more biblical content on the fatherless, which can be used in Bible studies and preaching.)

Embedding the Value

Borrowing from preaching jargon, values are embedded when they are brought, taught and caught—"brought" meaning the value is clearly spelled out, "taught" meaning the value requires clear articulation and "caught" implying the value is embraced by the community. Here are some practical ways you can begin the process of embedding a fatherless value in your church, ministry or organization.

1. Create an awareness of the value. Almost every church, ministry or organization has a clearly defined mission statement. The mission statement is written out and accessible for everyone to see. To create the awareness of a fatherless value, writing a value statement is a good place to start. If you are the pastor or leader, engage in this writing process with a group of strategic leaders in your church or ministry. This will allow them to begin to think about and wrap their hearts and minds around the importance of this value. You might conduct a few Bible studies on the topic or even suggest they read this book.

After an adequate time of education, engage in writing the value statement. The goal is not to write a novel but a simple statement that captures the ethos of what you want your church or ministry to embrace as it relates to fatherlessness. For example, your value statement might look something like this: According to James 1:27, Northeast Community Church values the scriptural mandate to care for the fatherless. We are committed to share God's grace to the fatherless by being sensitive to their needs and by engaging in tangible acts of service in order to enhance their lives through the love of Jesus Christ.

Your value statement will serve as a guiding principle for your church, ministry or organization. It will spur your thinking and dreaming mechanisms to be creative in addressing the need as well as making it a priority in your church.

Once your value statement has been crafted, you can begin to use it to create awareness in your church. Here are some ideas:

- Include it in your church membership classes, seminars or orientations.
- Place it on appropriate literature or brochures.
- Pass it out to members of your staff.
- Post it on a wall somewhere in your church where people can read it.
- Share it from the pulpit.
- Post it on your website, send out a tweet or put it on your Facebook page.
- Have a staff prayer meeting and pray over the value and its implementation.
- Write an article and include the statement, and email, blog or mail it to church members.

- Include it in a newsletter.

- Say it over and over again.

Communication is essential for creating awareness in your church, ministry or organization. (I won't go into detail here, because I explore in chapter four how to communicate to meet the needs of the fatherless.) However, it's important to note that the more widespread the communication, the deeper the value will be embedded in your church or ministry culture. The more you can talk, preach, share or facilitate conversation on the value, the better.

2. Create avenues for ministry. There is no need to try to create something new unless you want to or God instructs you to do so. The first order of the day then is to take inventory of your existing ministries or services. Identify what ministries and services function in your church—men's ministry, women's ministry, small groups, prayer meetings, children's ministry, single mothers and all others. After your assessment, determine how the value can be infused into each of them.

In our church, we have a number of ministries in which the fatherless value has been embedded. Two such ministries are Men of Destiny and the Prayer Ministry. Men of Destiny is our men's ministry, which of course does regular men things: eat, play, pray and study God's Word. A few times a year we go to a ballgame. Of course, we take our own children, but we make a big push to take kids who don't have a dad present. We encourage all the single moms to get their children signed up, and in most cases we tell them that they aren't required to pay.

The time at the game accomplishes a couple of things. One, everybody has a great time. The peanuts, popcorn and Cracker Jacks are a grand slam, and when our team wins, it's an extra bonus. Something else special also occurs: Sammy makes a connection with Brother Charles. Because there's a bond that begins to form because they spent time together, they start to have conversations at church with each other. Brother Charles is now more aware of Sammy's needs, and Sammy knows Brother Charles is there for him. We also have seen moms ask a brother to talk to or spend time with their son when he's going through a turbulent time. This happens due to the fatherless value that's woven into the fabric of Men of Destiny.

One Sunday morning, Malcolm saw me walking down the aisle of the sanctuary. He's a young man who has had his fair share of troubles, to say the least, and his father is absent. Uncharacteristically, when he saw me, he threw his arms around me and said God had deeply touched his life. He explained to me how he had genuinely experienced God's help and grace, and he conveyed a deep sense of gratitude as well.

I asked what had happened, and I learned that he had attended the Prayer Ministry a few days earlier. Our prayer leader told me how Malcom had come into the prayer time weighed down by all the issues going on in his life. Aware of his fatherlessness, she had instructed the prayer group to circle around him and pray. As they prayed, God showed up! The best way to explain it is God the Father embraced young Malcom and gave him the fatherly touch he so desperately needed. The women in this prayer group touched God the Father, and God the Father touched this fatherless young man.

I want to inject the importance of embedding the fatherless value in your ministry to single mothers and children. With the help of single mothers, figure out what you could do to make their load lighter. We have taken up offerings to help them financially, and the men's ministry bought one mom a car. We have special prayers for them. We want them to know we love and value them.

Fatherless children are in the classroom of your children's ministry. Make sure your curriculum teaches them that God is their father and that they are loved and valued even though Daddy isn't around. Have some of the men in the church help with some of the teaching and other activities. Being conscious of the need will help you devise ways to meet these children's vital need.

Identify the ministries in your church and make a few simple adjustments. You will be surprised how God can use what he has already given you to minister to the fatherless in your midst. Once the value is embedded, the ministries will create their own particular organic expressions to meet the need.

3. Give awards. In other words, celebrate the progress. Sometimes when dealing with an issue that's of the magnitude of fatherlessness, your efforts may seem to have no effect. However, with all diligence you must resist that notion. It's simply not true. Any service or helping hand you or your church extends is a blessing that will make a difference in an individual's life. Your efforts, no matter how big or small, deserve celebration.

Awards should and can be given in private and in public. Identify the people who are making a difference, and give them words of encouragement from time to time. Let them know that they are doing a great job and that their commitment and service honors God and blesses the lives of the fatherless in the church and community. You could also give them a small token of appreciation, such as a thank-you card or even a gift card to the local coffee shop. Send them an email and write a Scripture on it expressing the value of their service and their life. Most people who have a passion to serve don't require many pats on the back, but when you give them one, they enjoy it and it lasts for many miles.

Public awards are encouraging as well. Occasionally highlight those ministries in your church that have embraced the fatherless value and are doing creative ministry. Make others aware of the work they're doing so it doesn't go unnoticed. The young people in our church call this giving "props." Props can be given to a person or ministry during a church service. The time of recognition doesn't have to take up half the service; a couple of minutes suffices. Taking a moment to acknowledge a person or ministry makes the congregation aware and expresses appreciation on behalf of the church for their good work.

Giving props does more than validate the person. It reinforces to the congregation the priority of the value. It clarifies the message that ministry to the fatherless is a priority for your church. This can happen in other group contexts as well, such as staff meetings and small groups. The sky is the limit in terms of ways to give awards and celebrate the execution of the fatherless value. What is important is that you do it.

Changing a Life

Thomas grew up in a major city on the northeast coast of the United States, the only child of his mother's first marriage. Her second marriage to his stepfather and the five subsequent children were the only family he knew. It was a very dysfunctional family environment filled with violence and abuse on every level. Thomas explains: "My stepfather and mother had knockdown, drag-out fights on a regular basis, including weapons such as guns and knives. It was commonplace for my mother to chase my father through the house, shooting at him with a gun. With no exaggeration, their antics would not disrupt my siblings and me from eating our meal at the kitchen table. In our minds, it was just 'Momma and Daddy are fighting again.'"

Thomas's difficult setting extended beyond his home.

As a kid, I was exposed to people being murdered on a regular basis in gang, domestic and hustle-related violence. People were stabbed, shot, drowned, thrown off buildings and beaten to death, as life was a game. On the streets the measure of a man was determined by the hardness and callousness of his heart and soul. When I was sixteen years old, I beat and kicked the first girl I loved because she made me angry. I had to man up! After hurting her, I felt sick inside, but stepdad and the streets had shown me what a man looked like.

Thomas had learned how to be a man and a father from his stepfather by observation. He says, "A father impacts you whether they are intentionally engaged with you or not." He eventually came to follow Christ and is now studying in seminary to fulfill his call to preach. He found himself longing for a spiritual father figure, but didn't find that desire fulfilled.

> Some people are too busy with their own lives and don't have the time or desire to invest in the lives of others. Intimacy in church life and community can be messy at times, and people don't want the messy. Sunday-morning surface relationships are much simpler and not relationally complicated. But there was another reason: I lacked the spiritual father relationship. In my frustration and pain, God spoke to my heart and said, "Stop looking to others and look to me for what you need. Become that person for someone else."
>
> So now I am on a journey. Not an easy journey, but the right path. Where I was once hard, I found that the more broken and humble I am before God, the stronger I am. His strength is made perfect in my weakness. Where everything around me in the world says you have to take care of yourself and "get yours," I've found that the more I live to serve others, the more fulfilling my life is.

Thomas's life is a testimony to the power of God and the loving change he can bring into our lives as our Father, and it also reminds us of how many young men are longing for the church to fill in the gap in their lives.

A Fatherless Value Church

Pastor Ron Bronski is the lead pastor of Song of Hope Church in Vancouver, Washington. His approach to embedding the fatherless value is at the core of his mission, philosophy, vision and values. For him, the fatherless value was not an add-on, but a foundation to build on.

In 1987, Pastor Ron started the Song of Hope Church in one of the poorest areas in town. His target group was the disenfranchised children in that area. Out of the hundreds of kids he reached, 70 percent were in homes with either no father or an inept father. Song of Hope Church conducted Bible clubs, ran an extensive literacy program and reached out to and provided services to parents. Their church had such an impact that the local grade school would check to see if they were having an event; if Song of Hope was having an event and the school was holding an event on the same day, the school's chairs would be empty.

However, Pastor Ron and his wife, Debbie, went a step further than just offering wonderful services. They opened up their lives and home to the dozens of kids in their neighborhood. On Friday nights, they hosted sleepovers in their home. Many of the fatherless neighborhood kids would pile into the Bronski house and get the firsthand experience of what it would be like if dad were home. In addition, they took the kids on camping trips and fishing excursions, which allowed them to experience delights outside their broken world. In my book, Ron and Debbie are heroes. There are literally dozens of fatherless children who are doing well today because of what they deem valuable.

If you are planting a church, now is the time to think about this kind of ministry. Having served as a pastor for over twenty-four years, I can honestly tell you it's easier to place a rock in the foundation before the structure goes up than to place it once the structure is erected. When Pastor Ron started Song of Hope Church, he was clear that ministry to the poor, children and the fatherless would not just be a principle, but a guiding conviction.

If you're starting a ministry, allow the Lord to plant the fatherless value in your heart now. Make it a conviction for your ministry from the beginning. As your work grows, the value will grow in the hearts of the people you serve.

For the rest of us, we can take heart that the Lord will help us where we are. We aren't all called to be a Pastor Ron, nor do we all have the gifting and grace that is on his life. However, God can and will use you to embed a fatherless value in the place where you are serving. If you embed it, your church, organization or ministry can be a place where fatherless individuals can find a blanket with a "Big letter L."

4

GETTING THE MESSAGE OUT

A group of ten or so high school and college young folks was visiting our church from eastern Washington. The message that morning was on fatherlessness. After the message, a young Hispanic man came forward for prayer and literally poured his heart out to God. Several of his friends gathered around him and prayed with him. It was a beautiful sight to observe.

A few months later, I received a call from the pastor of the group, and he explained to me the miracle that had taken place in the young man's life. He had been in deep turmoil due to his relationship with his father—full of anger, depression and destructive tendencies. However, after he heard a message of God's love for him and God's desire to be his father, love reached his heart. The pastor said the young man was doing great; the transformation God worked in his heart that day was authentic. We have people visit our church all the time, but I seldom receive calls from visitors bearing such encouraging news.

Romans 10:14-15 articulates two essentials for communicating an important message: "How can they hear without someone preaching to them? And how can they preach unless they are sent?" Though this passage specifically addresses the propagation of the gospel, the ingredients apply for communicating the issue of fatherlessness as well.

First, these verses teach us that for people to believe a message, it first has to be communicated to them. Belief and action are a response to a conveyed message. No message equals no belief or action. Second, importance is placed on the messenger. How can they preach unless they have been sent? Being sent requires that the messenger possess an understanding that sharing a particular message is his or her responsibility and duty. The underlying assumption is that the messenger has been communicated to—in this case by God—in order to convey the message.

Simply stated, people in your church, organization or ministry benefit by being informed on the issue of fatherlessness. To make this happen, you as the pastor or leader must embrace the task of communicating the message.

By communicating the fatherless issue to your constituency, you inform, inspire and engage them to make a difference in the lives of the fatherless. Several ways you can communicate the issues and solutions to fatherlessness in your place of service are through preaching, personal conversations, publications, personal testimonies and projects.

Preaching

Preaching is one of the pastor's most strategic vehicles in helping to inspire, educate and mobilize a congregation for ministry to the fatherless. It's a powerful tool to help the church begin to wrap its arms around the issues surrounding father absenteeism. While some in the congregation may understand the nuances of father absenteeism on an experiential level, preaching allows you to enrich the conversation with sociological and psychological information placed within a biblical framework.

For example, someone suffers from a chronic pain in his neck.

Day after day the pain nags him. He doesn't know what the cause of the pain is; all he knows is that his neck hurts. Along the course of time, he picks up and reads a book that happens to have a chapter on chronic neck pain. As he reads the chapter, he realizes the symptoms he's experiencing are described to a tee in the book. He discovers that he is suffering from a pinched nerve. The pain was always there, but he was unaware of the diagnosis and what to do to remedy the situation.

Most people in your congregation are aware of the fatherless issue on a feeling level. But that's not enough. Information needs to be communicated so they understand what they are feeling and have strategies to remedy the situation. Preaching on the subject brings the needed knowledge and understanding to the church.

Through preaching, you can contextualize the issue of father absenteeism by articulating the problem in the vernacular of your own community. No one understands your ministry setting like you. You know what will fly and what will sink. You can craft your message in such a way that it rings a bell to your church or ministry. The core elements of the issue and its solutions are the same, but how you communicate is up to you. Be yourself and be authentic.

Preaching on father absenteeism should achieve the following goals:

- Educate the church on the problem of father absenteeism
- Make the church aware of the effects of father absenteeism on children
- Empower single mothers as individuals and parents
- Stress the importance of marriage as it relates to father absenteeism.
- Address the father's responsibility to his children

- Make the community aware of its responsibility to the fatherless

- Present God as the supreme Father for every person and child

To accomplish this preaching goal, I recommend preaching a sermon series covering various facets of the fatherlessness issue. The following is a template that could be used to achieve the goal.

WEEK ONE

Sermon title: Daddy, Where Are You?

Scripture: 1 Corinthians 4:15

Emphasis: Make the church aware of the father crisis. Discuss some of the causes (see chapter one) and give the *church* hope that they can be a part of the solution.

WEEK TWO

Sermon title: What Dad Leaves Behind When He Goes

Scripture: Jeremiah 31:29

Emphasis: Discuss the effects of father absenteeism on the children. Utilize portions of the data provided in chapter two of this book. Give hope, and encourage those in the congregation who may be suffering. Place on the minds of fathers the importance of staying close to their children.

WEEK THREE

Sermon title: God, the Single Mother's Secret Weapon

Scripture: Deuteronomy 10:18

Emphasis: Assure the single mom that she's not alone. Validate her and assure her that God and the church are standing with her. Give examples from Scripture of how God helped and strengthened single mothers in their time of need. Also encourage other segments of the church to be sensitive to the needs of single moms. They may be the vessels God uses to bring aid to single moms, and single moms may be the vessels God uses to bless them as well.

WEEK FOUR

Sermon title: Your Home, Something Worth Fighting For

Scripture: Nehemiah 4:14

Emphasis: Having a good marriage and raising kids present unique challenges. No matter how great the challenge, a home is worth fighting for. A husband and a wife staying together in a healthy manner is the best thing they can give to their children. Suggest tools to fight with, such as communication, love and prayer.

WEEK FIVE

Sermon title: Dads Who Play by the Rules

Scripture: Ephesians 6:4; Colossians 3:21

Emphasis: Discuss some of the responsibilities that Scripture requires fathers to fulfill. Use both Old and New Testament. Chapter five in this book, on the roles of a father, will be helpful.

WEEK SIX

Sermon title: Church, They're Your Kids Too

Scripture: James 1:27

Emphasis: Explain to the church its God-given responsibility to minister to the fatherless. Create a case using the Old and New Testaments and give some practical ways the church can get involved. It may be good at this juncture to have the task force share its plan of action with the church and then validate it as the pastor, giving the church the charge to get moving.

WEEK SEVEN

Sermon title: We Call Him Father

Scripture: Matthew 5:45–7:21 (Choose the verses that talk about the attributes of God as Father.)

Emphasis: Not everyone has had a positive experience with her or his father. Many men have given fatherhood a bad name. In this sermon, stress that God is a good father who loves and cares for his children in a way that is superior to and beyond any earthly father. You want to proclaim that he is a father who is trustworthy and reliable (see chapter eight, "God Our Father").

At the conclusion of this series on fathering the fatherless, the church should have a good overview of the issue of father absenteeism and also understand that they have a responsibility to act and make a difference in the lives of those whose dads are missing. The issue of fatherlessness is not going to vanish; therefore, you have to preach on the topic repeatedly. The sermons listed above could easily be expanded for future preaching on the subject.

One Sunday after I had preached a sermon along these lines, I gave an appeal to those who had been affected by fatherlessness to come to the altar for prayer and support. To my amazement, the altar was flooded with people. Young adults, some seniors, small children and teenagers were all present. As I looked at the faces of the people, many were covered with tears; others were in a state of contemplation. As we prayed, some began to sob. It was as if pain that had been dormant or intentionally hidden had surfaced and was allowed to be released.

Many people went home changed that day because a deep-seated need was touched by the Spirit of God. Many were able to open up and talk about their pain with others. After that service, I had one mother come to me and say how much she appreciated it because her child had been holding all the hurt and anger in, and she couldn't get her to open up and talk; after that service, she began talking. Individuals in the congregation also became more aware and sensitive to those around them who were grappling with the effects of fatherlessness.

If your preaching schedule prevents you from doing a whole service, I find that other opportunities to raise awareness of fatherlessness—its causes, prevention and opportunities—are effective as well. You can slip in thoughts on marriage, dads spending time with their children, the need for mentors and surrogate fathers, the importance of prayer and so on. Take a minute or thirty seconds to inject a fatherless message. Someone will hear it.

On many occasions I also speak to the children and young people from the pulpit as if I were talking to my own sons or daughters. Sadly, for some, the only fatherly voice they hear is mine. Here's a story that explains my point: I'm always preaching to my son about his work ethic around the house. As a young man focused on everything he does outside the home, he's also convinced that his work around the house is a substantial necessity. According to his belief system, he does *everything*. In fact, on one occasion he told his aunt he failed to see how our house would continue to operate smoothly when he went away to college, because his contribution was so vital. I wanted to ask my sister, is he trying to be like Steve Harvey or Conan O'Brien?

Anyway, I know there are a number of kids and teens sitting in the congregation with the same misconstrued belief system as my son. So, one Sunday I took a little detour and talked a few minutes about my childhood and how my dad made us work on projects from landscaping to roofing. If work was required in the Strong house, we did it. I interjected this fatherly speech to the kids with some humor and framed it in the understanding that this is what I tell my kids. I gave them the same speech I have repeatedly preached to my son.

I told them directly, "You guys know your mom works hard to support you, and you have a responsibility to help around the house. What you do at home and your attitude there will affect how you do elsewhere in life. Besides, we thank you for what you do around the house, but you need to understand that it's your reasonable service."

Following this Sunday's message, I was having lunch with a young man whose mom had graduated to heaven and whose father was absent. He was leaving for school in a couple of days. I asked him how things were going and what he'd been doing the last week. He responded by saying that some contractors were working on their house, and he was too. Then he asked, "Pastor Mark, you know that sermon you preached about growing up and having to work?"

I replied, "Yep."

"Well, my sister had me staining the deck because of what you preached. She told me I didn't have the privilege of lying around the house and doing nothing, so stain the deck." He moaned about working in the hot sun and how long it took, but he did it.

Be cognizant of the reality that many kids in your congregation won't hear any fatherly advice except yours. With this in mind, share your heart and wisdom; it will be appreciated. Let your pulpit be a place where the cry of the fatherless can be heard and the fatherless can hear.

Personal Conversations

Some of the most transformative moments in my life have not come from listening to a sermon, but in moments of a simple conversation with another person. I've made life-changing decisions after conversing with a friend. When I was working on my doctorate, my life was in a vice. My wife was several months pregnant, our church was in the middle of an extensive building renovation, my traveling schedule was hectic, and I was going to school. Besides that, I had just had an extensive personality analysis, and the counselor had told me I was burned out and needed to quit not only school, but everything else too.

One night while we were at a spiritual retreat, I woke up at three in the morning and said, "That's it. I'm dropping out of the program today." I had made up my mind that when the rooster crowed, my school days would be officially over. But before the rooster crowed, I had a conversation with my previous pastor and good friend, Jack Jaffe. As we talked, I told him my plans, and he just listened. At the end of the conversation, he said, "Friend, it sounds to me like God is trying to work something out in your life and your flesh doesn't appreciate it."

After our conversation, I didn't feel better, but I changed my mind and stayed in the program. Through much prayer effort and work, I finished school, we had our baby, we moved into our house, and I finished my travel commitments. The point of this detour is, conversations have the power to affect the direction of a life. My conversation with Jack impacted my life and my future.

As a leader, you have the opportunity to converse with many people. Don't become like a product salesperson who constantly hawks the best item in the universe. Strategically use conversations to raise awareness and inspire people to develop a heart for action on behalf of the fatherless.

In your conversations, avoid relaying only facts; talk about the fatherless kids in your church and community. Mention them by name in cases when confidentiality isn't an issue. Help people see their faces and see their hearts. Take moments when engaging in those conversations to pray. Pray for the fathers, the single mothers and the children. Encourage people to allow God to use them in this area. Take time to listen too. One conversation you engage in may ignite the heart of a person who will champion the fatherless cause in your church or community.

Personal Testimonies

Personal testimonies are stories about people's life and journey. Stories have the ability to move an individual to a new place of truth. Jesus was a master at using stories to communicate kingdom truth. He told stories about nature, stories about people and stories about life. People were transformed then and countless individuals are still transformed by the parables he spoke. You have powerful stories sitting in the pews of your church right now.

I would venture to say you have people in your congregation

who have grown up without a father and have experienced the repercussions of that void. Or there are people who are still in the throes of the battles but are overcoming the struggle by the grace of God. These people can communicate a much-needed word to your congregation.

Cory is an awesome young man at our church with a great heart and a powerful redemptive testimony. He told me he was conceived on a Christmas Eve, when his mother went out and cheated on her boyfriend. That night was not as cut and dry as it may seem. Even though his mom knew the night he was conceived, she doesn't know who the man was. So to this day, Cory doesn't know who his biological father is.

From the cradle to six years of age, Cory saw it all: alcoholism, drug usage, illicit sex and every other kind of ill. His life was a revolving door as he went in and out of rehab with his mother. When Cory turned nine, she gave birth to his baby sister. For a few years, she stayed sober, but then the mayhem began again. This time, along with the drug usage, she had stints in jail as well as in rehab. By the time Cory was twelve, he had experimented with everything he had been exposed to. The situation grew so dire with his mother that he and his sister went to live with his uncle.

A few years later, a pastor who had kids his age moved in next door to him. After observing Cory's lifestyle, one of the pastor's sons said to him, "I'm scared for your life; you need to come to church with us." He agreed to go and made a commitment to Jesus Christ. But the commitment didn't stick. According to Cory, he had no foundation to build on, so off he slid again, back into a destructive lifestyle. Cory even had a scholarship to go to school, but he lost it because of excessive partying.

Fast-forward. Over the last five years, Christ has drastically changed Cory's life. He has completed our discipleship program and Leadership Institute. He is a leader in our young-adult ministry, he has a lovely wife, and he's back in school.

Cory's story is powerful. His testimony is a great source of hope to young people and children who are struggling not just with father absenteeism but with mother abandonment as well. His testimony gives a vivid portrayal of how deep the pain and dysfunction runs. His story tells listeners how important it is for moms and dads to fulfill their parental responsibilities. Finally, it shows the power of God to restore broken lives that have been mishandled by parents.

Libraries of stories are in your church. These testimonies are a wealth of inspiration and information to move your congregation to a new place of truth about how the church can minister to the fatherless. Utilize people in your church, giving them space to give their testimonies. The stories they communicate will speak to the heart of those that hear.

Projects

Every year my wife and Trina Polk lead a gift drive called The Angel Tree for kids whose parents are incarcerated. Of course, more fathers are incarcerated than mothers. This project affords our church with a couple of opportunities. Just sharing the nature of the project creates an awareness of how many children in our community are without a dad.

Every year we have dozens of names of children on the tree. My wife and Trina encourage members of the congregation to pick a name off the tree and make that Christmas special for that child. It amazes me how many people participate. Sometimes I see people in our church who don't have great financial means choosing to help these children. Our church members throw themselves into the project.

Others churches have embarked on other projects. City Harvest Church in Vancouver, Washington, adopted an apartment complex and has served the tenants by cleaning, cooking, painting or whatever their hands find to do. The impact they had was so phenomenal, it was featured on the local news.

Doing a project allows more people to see the need firsthand. It also provides them the satisfaction of being able to make a difference in the lives of people. Most churches conduct mission trips. This usually includes education on the nuances of the mission site. Money is raised to support and send the team or missionaries. Prayers are made for God's blessing to avail on the efforts. The whole church is engaged and excited that "our church is going on a mission trip." The same mileage can be gained by conducting a project to meet the needs of the fatherless in your city or church.

I encourage you to look also within the four walls of your church. You may have a number of struggling single mothers who are in desperate need of help. Pull a creative team together who can develop a one-day project that brings blessing to those mothers and their children. Ultimately your church will be more sensitized to the fatherless issue and be more readily able to serve in the future.

Publications

Finally, utilizing various media outlets is a great way to communicate the fatherless issue to your church. The National Fatherhood Initiative has many useful resources for creating fatherless and prevention awareness in your church. You could place brochures on the subject in your church information corner. If you have a bookstore or information table, place a book or two on fatherlessness there.

In the children's wing of our church, my wife made a collage of the children's pictures on the wall, with a heading "Wall of Prayer: Praying for our Children." Some of the children have dads, but many do not. Every time members of the congregation walk into the children's wing, they are reminded to pray for our kids.

Creating PowerPoint presentations, prayer cards, posters and even commercials are all helpful ways to get the message out. Be creative as you utilize the media vehicles you already have in your church. The goal is not overload, but beaming enough light to create a healthy awareness. The goal isn't to make a splash, though there's nothing wrong with a huge splash every now and then. A constant trickle week by week, month by month, year by year will have the greatest impact. Using publications helps with that goal. Just turn the faucet on a bit.

To curb the effects of fatherlessness, the issue must be communicated to the church. How can they hear without a preacher? They can't. How can he preach unless he has been sent? He won't go. The good news is, you will communicate and share the issue because you have been sent to do the job. Your feet are beautiful. And your church will hear and act.

5

EQUIPPING MEN TO BE FATHERS

A few years ago, I conducted a funeral at another church in our city. It was gut-wrenching due to the circumstances surrounding the young man's death. The church was packed wall to wall with grieving young people attempting to make sense of a needless and so final occurrence. The deceased young man had been involved in gangs. I gathered from some of the comments of the adults that he felt trapped; he didn't see any way out of his lifestyle.

When I finished the eulogy, the funeral directors opened the casket so that friends and family could say their final farewells. What usually follows is standard fair: tears are shed, words of good-bye are spoken, and stares into the heavens are made. But during this viewing, I experienced something I'd never witnessed before. A tall, well-dressed man came and stood over the casket, and stared. After standing there for what seemed like an extremely long time, he removed the tie from his neck and placed it on his dead son. He then went back to his seat. Moments passed, and he proceeded to the casket once again. This time, while standing there, he took off his watch and placed it on his deceased son's wrist. If my memory serves me correctly, he also removed a chain from his neck and placed it on the young man. This father grieving over his son puzzled me. It seemed bizarre that he would place these objects on his son.

After the service, a woman who was like the boy's mother told me what was going on. In fact, she's the one who informed me that the man was the boy's father. She made clear to me in no uncertain terms that this dad had not been a parent to the young man; he had been out of his life for the most part.

Then it hit me: this father wasn't dealing with grief alone, but with guilt as well. In placing those useless objects on his son's cold body, he was trying to fulfill his fatherly duties in a pitiful way. Of course, he was too late. The questions I ask myself are, why didn't he give his son a tie and teach him how to tie it when he was nine or ten? How come he didn't give his son a Mickey Mouse watch and teach him how to tell time when he was still in grade school? What kept this man from being a father to his son? I'm sure there are a number of contributing factors to his failure, but one plausible answer is that he didn't know how.

Learning to Be a Father

My friend and mentor Bob was born into a family of Italian descent. He told me a powerful story concerning him and his father. When his father was a boy, his dad was an abusive and hard man. Bob says on one occasion his grandfather beat his grandmother to a bloody pulp. As a result, Bob's dad grew up unable to receive fatherly love and affection from his father. According to Bob, his father would become angry at the drop of the hat. While he was growing up, his father never told him on any occasion that he loved him.

Bob had a brother who died never having heard those precious words from his father's lips. After this son's death, and at age seventy-five, Bob's dad bowed to God and asked him for help. One week later, he went to Bob, then forty-plus years old, and told him for the first time that he loved him. Bob was overwhelmed.

Before his dad's graduation to heaven, he told Bob he loved him every day, and he showed affection and tenderness to the grandchildren and great-grandchildren in abundance. What this story teaches us is that fathers *can* become better fathers and that it's never too late to change.

By educating, we can encourage our fathers to change sooner, for the better. Our society teaches our boys how to play ball, how to invest money, how to be tough, but not how to be fathers. Traditionally a boy could learn how to be a father by watching his own dad, but now, with the problem of father absenteeism, boys sit in the classroom of life with no father teacher.

Equipping men to be fathers is imperative in combating fatherlessness. If men genuinely understand what's required of them as fathers and are equipped with the necessary skills and tools, the pain for many fatherless kids will subside.

Understanding this, our churches ministries and organizations must be intentional in equipping men to fulfill their God-given roles as fathers. We must address crucial questions: What are the roles and responsibilities of a father? Is he just to be present, or also be the provider? Is his main job to be a disciplinarian? Does his treatment of his wife have any bearing on his relationship with his kids? Does he need to show emotional support to his children? The list goes on, but it's necessary to have a clear and concise description of what a father is to be. The Scriptures provide us with a more than adequate blueprint for being and for equipping good fathers. By no means is the following summary exhaustive, but it highlights aspects from the Old and New Testament to help us in our quest.

Roles of Fathers in the Old Testament
One Old Testament role of the earthly father is the redemption of

the firstborn, an example of which is found in Genesis 22, where Abraham is instructed by God to take his one and only son whom he loves and offer him up as a sacrifice. In his book *Biblical Faith and Fathering*, John Miller states that offering one's firstborn son to God as an act of devotion was a widespread practice in antiquity.[1] Many worshippers of various pagan religions considered it a moral responsibility to offer to their gods their firstborn son as a sacrifice to prove their devotion. It should be pointed out here, however, that human sacrifices had no place in God's plan.

Exodus, like Genesis, emphasizes the redemption of the firstborn (Ex 12:21-34; 13:11-16). However, Exodus places a different spin on the Abrahamic sacrifice ritual. When the child asks the father what the meaning of the sacrifice is, the father responds theologically to his son by explaining the activity of God in the lives of his people. Concerning this shift, Miller says,

> In other words, through this ritual the hard won insight (already embodied in the story of Abraham's near sacrifice of his first-born), that God wants our devotion not that we kill our sons, was brought to dramatic, confessional experience here, however, within the framework of the story of Israel's liberation from Egypt. Just as the tragic death of Egypt's first-born was ritually alluded to in the offering up of the first-born of the flocks, so the memory of the redemptive preservation of Israel's first-born during the same sequence of events was kept alive by the rite of the son's release. In this way the truth was dramatized that Israel's God is a "redemptive father" (Is 63:16) whom Israelite fathers should emulate in the care of their children.[2]

In Judaism, the act of redemption is still performed today. On the child's thirty-first day, he is brought to the rabbi in the presence of family and guests. When the father approaches the altar with the child, he is asked if he desires to leave the child or redeem him. If the father chooses to redeem the child, he hands a special coin to the rabbi, and the rabbi pronounces three times in the presence of the company of people, "Your son is redeemed." Afterward the child is returned to the father.

The implications of this ritual are riveting. For one, the father publicly acknowledges that he accepts full responsibility for his son before God and the people. Second, the son grows up knowing that his dad publicly chose him and redeemed him. Knowing that he has a father who wanted him and chose him has great spiritual, emotional and psychological implications throughout the child's life.

In an age when many children don't even have a father's name on their birth certificates, the importance of this ritual can't be underestimated. Children need to know that Daddy loves them, not simply because of biological responsibility, but because they have great value in and of themselves. The redemption rite says to the child, "My father wants me, and he is not ashamed to tell the world." Communicating this love is a responsibility that no father can afford to neglect. As long as a father is able, he must tell his child, "You are mine; I love you and I want you." The time to begin the message is when the child is born.

Circumcision is another ritual that highlights the importance of the father-son relationship. We will discuss this in greater detail in chapter seven. However, it's important to note here that circumcision mandated the father to mark his son for God's sake. The cutting away of the flesh would be a reminder to the child that he was a part of God's covenant. The father's role was essential for making that mark of demarcation. A father's contributions today are essential for helping establish their children's spiritual life.

Finally, Miller discusses the rite of the Passover as it relates to fatherhood. The Passover feast was one of the most celebrated in the Israelite community. Its origins are in the exodus of Israel from Egypt (Ex 12:1–13:6). Prior to their departure, the Israelites were required to sacrifice a lamb and spread the blood over the doorpost so that God would pass over each home and not destroy their firstborn as he would the firstborn of the Egyptians. They were also instructed to eat unleavened bread. The absence of the yeast in the bread was because they would not have time to prepare the bread as usual with their rapid departure from Egypt.

Fathers played an important role in the context of the Passover celebration. In preparation for the Passover, they were required to select, kill and roast the animals. They were also required to smear the blood over the doorpost. Passover is unique in that it was not only a male-to-male ritual; it involved the entire household—wives and daughters as well as sons. Through the Passover meal, the family was gathered within the confines of the four walls of their home. They ate a meal together that had enormous theological meaning and fatherhood significance.

The father was to function in a priestly role by saying a prayer with the family and explaining the theological significance of the meal to them all. In relation to the significance of the father, Miller writes,

> Just as Yahweh acted for salvation, so does the father. He too must save his family from destructive forces that threaten it. While Yahweh is the ultimate redeemer, the father must act too (if their families are not to perish) by gathering their families around them within the intimacy of the four walls of their respective houses.[3]

He concludes by underscoring the importance of Passover and the father's role in the celebration:

> No other ritual drama plays as forcefully as does this one the interplay between God the father and the Israelite father in the care of his children. It is the culmination and embodiment of the other two rituals. If the redemption of the first-born and circumcision are adoption rituals initiating the father as custodian, guide of his sons in particular,

Passover expands that role, year after year and makes it visible and accessible to the whole family. Through it fathers in Israel, as in no other culture we know of, appropriated to themselves an identity as redemptive caretakers, with permanent stake in the life of their families.[4]

The Passover speaks deeply into our society's current father drought. Namely, if the father is to function as a redemptive caretaker, it helps a great deal for him to be present in the home. If the father is absent, it's much harder for him to have the intimacy and teaching opportunities with his children that he would have if he were eating a daily meal within the four walls of his home with his little ones. The Passover teaches fathers today that they are to be close to their children, or present. It teaches that they are to provide resources not only for their children's natural needs, but also for their spiritual ones. Fathers are to work to maintain the continuity of their homes, because the home is a hallowed classroom in which to teach their children about the salvation of God.

The role of teacher is another important function of fathers in the Old Testament. The parental teaching mandate is articulated clearly in Deuteronomy 6:1-9. The father and mother were to teach their children in a cooperative effort (Prov 1:8; 23:22; 31:26). Regarding the Old Testament teaching model, Miller states, "This particular model requires a home where both the father and mother are present and both are completely familiar and at ease with the religious heritage, so they can share it in an informal, relaxed and friendly manner in the course of daily life."[5]

It goes without saying that the marriage union is crucial for such education to occur. From God's perspective, a married and present father is more effective in teaching his child than an absent one. The implication of this God-given role is straightforward. A father and a mother are to assume full responsibility as the principal teachers concerning God. To teach his child about God, a father has the responsibility first to live the Word and then to teach it. Part of living the Word is having a good marriage with the child's mother.

The redemption rite, circumcision, Passover and teaching all speak volumes in addressing the children's needs and the father's responsibilities. Essentially, these rites show that children need to have a sense of belonging (redemption rite); they need to be influenced in a godly fashion (circumcision); they need provision for their natural and spiritual life (Passover); and they need to be instructed in the ways of the Lord (teaching). As the father fulfills his responsibility, the children's needs will be met.

The attributes of God and the responsibilities that fathers were expected to perform in the various rituals in the Old Testament provide an excellent job description for today's fathers to follow.

New Testament Roles for Fathers

While there are a number of principles in the New Testament that indirectly give insight into the roles of fathers, I want to address two verses that speak directly to the role of earthly fathers with their children. They are Colossians 3:21, "Fathers, do not embitter your children, or they will become discouraged," and Ephesians 6:4, "Fathers, do not exasperate your children; instead, bring them up in the training and instruction of the Lord."

In the first part of these commands, fathers are instructed to control their anger and not drive their children to a point of frustration. In an age when abuse and domestic violence run rampant, this is a virtue that fathers should and must embrace. Some fathers do use anger as a device to control and as a means to force their children into conformity. This is not "cool." Anger and frustration are not the virtues for raising healthy children.

The implication of the verse is that a child thrives in an encouraging environment, not a hostile one. For that environment to be encouraging, the father must manage his emotions and behaviors himself, so he can properly influence and instruct his child in a healthy manner.

Ephesians 6:4 encourages fathers to play a significant role in the education of their children. This command goes against the idea of the father being simply the breadwinner in the home. God expects the father to be actively involved in his children's lives by providing guidance and teaching them to serve and to follow the ways of the Lord. Fathers should then be their children's chief spiritual adviser, pastor or whatever term you want to use. As Solomon in the Proverbs gave wisdom to his son, fathers are to do the same. However, the instruction should not be in word only; their lives are to be congruent with what they teach their children. The expectation is not for the father to be perfect, but to be authentic. The father mantra then is: do as I say and do as I do, and when you fail, admit it and regroup.

Though marriage is not mentioned directly as one of the roles of fathers, the Scriptures present marriage as the only legitimate vehicle for procreation. In Ephesians 5:22–6:3, the context of a father's role toward his children is marriage; husbands are instructed to love their wives. Though my grandfather was not a theologian or a Bible scholar, he gave me some advice that I believe is pertinent to this issue. He always said to me, "You can love your kids by the way you treat and love their mother, your wife." In other words, if you keep your marriage intact, the kids will have the benefit of a father and mother, both of which they need. One role of the father is to seek continually the health and well-being of his marriage.

In the New Testament, God is portrayed as a good father who provides for the needs of his children. He is a father who blesses his children in a context of a loving and intimate relationship. His character reflects his faithfulness, continuing presence, mercy, love, knowledge of his children's lives and ability to provide.

All of these attributes are to be emulated by earthly fathers as we care for our children. It is God's intent that natural fathers raise their children in a loving, harmonious relationship as well. In the context of a natural father's relationship with his children, he is expected to be a teacher, a provider and an encourager to his children. To do all of the above, he must be present. According to the New Testament, God the Father is our model, and by his grace we are to emulate him and be present in our children's lives.

Scripture Summary

The Old and New Testaments leave no room for speculation or assumption concerning the role of fathers. The biblical data states unequivocally that the father's role is essential and integral for the development of every dimension of a child's life. Fathering, therefore, is not simply biologically fathering a child, but requires that the father take an active part in raising the child as well.

Hence, the Scriptures clearly articulate the attributes a father should possess, and they show the responsibilities he is to fulfill in the life of his children. When fathers neglect their responsibilities, children suffer—and in many cases great needs are left unmet. The following chart sums up the biblical roles and necessary character attributes for fathers. It also highlights the needs of children and shows how those needs are met when fathers fulfill their roles.

Having gained a Scriptural understanding of the roles of fathers, now we can isolate the areas where men require equipping to be good fathers.

Equipping Fathers

According to the chart, there are nine biblical characteristics/ attributes a father should possess in order to meet the needs of his children. These traits also help us to identify the areas we can focus on to equip men to be good fathers.

- Equipping men to be loving fathers to their children

BIBLICAL OVERVIEW OF FATHERS' RESPONSIBILITIES AND CHILDREN'S NEEDS	
ROLES AND ATTRIBUTES OF FATHERS	*NEEDS OF CHILDREN*
Be loving, faithful and merciful. *Imitate the attributes of God in the Old and New Testaments.*	The need to feel treasured and loved. The need for emotional security and well-being.
Embrace and model justice. *Understand the concept theologically and model it behaviorally.*	The need for moral upbringing and guidance.
Assume full responsibility for their children. *Redemption rite, Paul's exposé on adoption into the family of God.*	The need for a sense of identity and belonging, to be a part of a loving family and community.
Provide for their children's needs. *Passover, the model of God as a providing father.*	The need for provisions flowing out of a relationship with a father who is accessible and present.
Educate and train their children to function effectively in society. *Passover and Old and New Testament mandates given to fathers.*	The need for instruction and teaching to develop life skills.
Aid their child in developing their relationship with God. *Circumcision, Passover, teaching responsibility.*	The need to be taught about God so they can develop their own relationship with God the Father.
Provide discipline, encouragement and accountability. *Old and New Testament exhortations.*	The need for boundaries and accountability.
Model a godly life for the child to follow. *Mentoring.*	The need for a tangible godly father (male) role model.
Form and maintain the marriage bond with their children's mother. *Old and New Testament exhortations, unity and dependency.*	The need for security and the benefit of having both a father and mother in the home.

Figure 1

- Equipping men to be moral guides for their children
- Equipping men to assume full responsibility for their children
- Equipping men to be providers for their children
- Equipping men to teach basic life skills to their children
- Equipping men to aid their children in their spiritual growth
- Equipping men to set appropriate boundaries for their children
- Equipping men to live a Christ-centered life before their children
- Equipping men to honor the child's mother

Equipping men to be loving fathers to their children. The rhyme asks the question "What are little boys made of?" The answer: frogs, snails and puppy dog tails. If that's our substance in our tender years, what are men made of now?

Let's face it, the males of our species are not noted for their tender hands and compassionate hearts. In fact, society in general is not rewarding of such male traits and characteristics. In our culture, the macho man receives the accolades and applause, not the tender man. Yes, men should be masculine. However, in our masculinity there should be aqueducts of love, mercy and faithfulness. These virtues should especially flow from a father's heart in abundance toward his children.

The existing reality dictates that showing love, mercy and faithfulness is not automatic. That's why we see child abuse, neglect, abandonment and all of the other ills that stem from an empty father reservoir. Fathers require training to express love, mercy and faithfulness effectively to their children. They don't just acquire theses skills and virtues by osmosis. Transmission has to come from some source, whether it's a Scripture they read, a lesson they learn, a model they watch or a book they read. As fathers grow in love, they can meet the need of their child to feel treasured, loved, emotionally secure and healthy.

Equipping men to be moral guides for their children. Malachi 6:8 says, "He has showed you, O man, what is good. And what does the LORD require of you? To act justly and to love mercy and to walk humbly with your God." Children need moral upbringing and guidance. They should receive a moral compass as a gift from their father. For more than a fair share of children, the gift never reaches their person. Some fathers can't teach them what is good because they themselves do not know what is good. They have never learned about biblical ethics and values, moral rights and wrongs, absolutes and so forth. You can't give what you don't have. Because many fathers lack a compass, they can't give a working compass to their children. In this case, the need for equipping is at a premium.

Equipping men to assume full responsibility for their children. Sad to say, large numbers of children in our society don't even know who their fathers are. Countless children don't have a father's name on their birth certificate. Responsibility for a child means that a father acknowledges that the child is his and that he is proud and grateful to God for such a gift. Responsibility means that the child's well-being isn't the responsibility solely of the mother or grandparents, but rests on his shoulders as well. Responsibility means you walk with your children down life's road and you do all that's in your ability to help them reach their destination. As fathers grow in fulfilling their responsibility, their children have a greater sense of identity and belonging, and they experience the warmth of a loving family and community.

Equipping men to be providers for their children. Fathers should provide for their children. Statistic show that in 2007 only 63.7 percent of mothers who were due child support received it.[6] Another chronic ailment that plagues our culture is men living off women. Yes, the economy is rough and jobs are scarce, but some of this was occurring when the economy was fine. For some men, it's not an economic issue, but a heart issue.

I remember talking to a guy my age who had a good job and was belly-aching because his son's mother asked him for money to buy the kid a new pair of shoes. He complained that he gave her a few hundred dollars a month ago already, so why didn't she buy him some shoes with that money? I guess he expected me to feel sorry for him, but in my mind, that is his reasonable service. There are a lot of fathers needing a change of heart who could greatly benefit from some training on providing for their children. Even if they lack the financial resources at this time, they still can possess the desire to be a provider.

Equipping men to teach their basic life skills to their children. Life skills are essential: knowing how to conduct yourself in public, knowing how to speak and relate to other people, understanding how to take of yourself—your health, hygiene and diet. These are skills that a father who is in close proximity to his children can impart to them. Fathers can be instructed how to enter their child's world and teach skills that will enable them to function as healthy social beings.

Equipping men to aid their children in their spiritual growth. One of the most important passages in the Bible reads,

> One of the teachers of the law came and heard them debating. Noticing that Jesus had given them a good answer, he asked him, "Of all the commandments, which is the most important?"
>
> "The most important one," answered Jesus, "is this: 'Hear, O Israel, the Lord our God, the Lord is one. Love the Lord your God with all your heart and with all your soul and with all your mind and with all your strength.' The second is this: 'Love your neighbor as yourself.' There is no commandment greater than these." (Mk 12:28-31)

Fathers have the unique privilege of helping their children to love God and others. They have many opportunities to aid in the spiritual develop and maturing of their child. For many children, Mom is the sole person who fulfills this role. This shouldn't be the case, because fathers are required to get in the game as well. Their children are ready for them to step up to the plate, swing the bat and help deepen their relationship to God. Equipping men in this area can help them to hit a home run in their child's life.

Equipping men to set appropriate boundaries for their children. Men can help their children set good life boundaries by providing encouragement, accountability and discipline. Effective fathering requires dads to have a fully equipped tool belt with the necessary tools to encourage and discipline their children. There are proper ways to encourage a child and improper ways. For example, I know a person who in most cases rewards his child with a big bag of candy. Yummy—yep! However, this is not always appropriate. Same goes with discipline; every incident is not worthy of the same severity of punishment. Fathers can greatly benefit from learning skills to help them be journeymen encouragers and disciplinarians.

Equipping men to live a Christ-centered life before their children. A father living as an authentic Christian before his children is worth more than millions. There is no substitute for the blessing and power that's released into children's lives as they witness their dad living for Jesus Christ. Men need to be challenged, encouraged and strengthened regularly to live a Christ-centered life. I know I do! Providing a vehicle that allows men to share their defeats and victories, woes and "I don't knows" is essential for their walk with Christ. Giving them a place where they can pray, be transparent and learn the Word of God helps them to be the model their children can look up to.

Equipping men to honor the child's mother. As I mentioned earlier, one of the best ways a dad can positively influence his child is by honoring the child's mother. Maintaining a healthy marriage is key, and healthy marriages take work. I always tell our congregation, "A marriage may be made in heaven, but it's worked out on earth!" Lasting marriages require continual skill building and the commitment to hang in there. Helping fathers strengthen their marriage enables them to hold the mother in a place of honor before their child. In the case of fathers who aren't married to the child's mother, strategic lessons can be learned and carried out to honor her in the eyes of her children. Fathers need equipping in knowing the importance of honoring their children's mother and in how to do it.

Equipping Strategies

Creating a delivery system for equipping fathers doesn't have to be complex. I'm a proponent of adequately meeting the need but keeping structures simple. Don't feel as if you have to create a monumental edifice to equip men to be fathers. Keep it simple and make it fun. Here are a few suggestions.

Start a small group for the fathers in your church or community. Small groups are fantastic ways to effect change and equip men. Set your objectives for what you want the group to accomplish. Define the rules of the group: confidentiality, respect, nonjudgmental attitudes and so on. You could develop your own study outline using the nine equipping points we just mentioned. Or you could use some of the very good resources that I'll recommend in a moment. There are also people in your church, organization and community who are knowledgeable on fatherless issues. Use them as a resource, such as having them share with the group from time to time. Set the day and the time the group will meet, and determine the duration. Identify people in your church who have a burden for this, give them the support, and turn them loose.

The beauty of a small group is that the men learn not just from what the curriculum teaches, but also from their interactions with one another. Also, the group serves as a support and accountability mechanism, increasing the chances of follow-through. Simple and doable.

Start a class. Just as you would hold a Bible class on learning how to pray, hold one on learning how to be a good dad. During your regular Bible study time, on a Wednesday night or during the Sunday school hour, insert a fatherhood class for nine to twelve weeks. Have the men bring their notepads, Bible and pens, and allow them to learn in a classroom setting how to be a good father.

Utilize your men's and women's ministry. In our men's and women's ministry, we've used a few books that have been a great help to the fatherless problem. Our men and women love to study a good book over a several-week time period. In your men's ministry, the men might pray over the issue, study the issue, and talk about the issue. Fathers already attend the ministry, and the topic is a natural fit. Not only would the men be better equipped, but they would also have the ability to help and strengthen other men in their circles—in the church and workplace, for example—who need to be better fathers. In the women's ministry, help them understand the importance of mothering as well as fathering. Give the single moms resources to help their child in case the father is absent. (See appendix A for additional resources.)

Equipping men to be good fathers is crucial in combating fatherlessness. Devise a plan for your church or organization, and keep it simple. The most important thing is to start somewhere. Your church can make a difference.

Start where you are, and many children will thank you.

6

MENTORING THE FATHERLESS

Growing up without his mother and father, and being shuffled like the shoe on a Monopoly board from house to house in the foster care system, Jay was plagued with mountainous issues. He bore a societal brand across his forehead, reading, "This one is doomed for failure." The message was so visible that everywhere he turned, whether in school or in the street, voices made sure he lived up to his branding.

For him, school was a disastrous endeavor. He constantly got into confrontations with teachers. Regularly he walked the hall to the office to be placed on suspension for a few days. His behavior was somewhat tolerated because he was labeled as having a developmental delay. So, the saga was ongoing—and expected. Complicating Jay's troubles was his addiction to drugs and alcohol.

Due to his misconduct, Jay was ordered to participate in a mentoring program led by a passionate Christian woman named Michelle. The At Promise program provides mentoring support to at-risk youth aged twelve to eighteen. She has recruited a number of godly men from throughout the city to mentor the boys by providing social activities, group interaction time and spiritual direction.

One day Jay's mentor, John, received a call from Jay in the midst of one of his tirades. John went to the school to talk with him. Jay told him, "I'm sick of people telling me I'll never make it or graduate from high school." John listened to him and let him know that his behavior justified many of the comments and remarks he was receiving. In essence, he explained to him that if he wanted to be treated different, he'd have to remove the brand from his forehead.

When telling me this story, Michelle enthusiastically exclaimed to me, "I saw the light come on in Jay's eyes. I could see it!" From the moment of that conversation with his mentor, Jay changed. And he set a goal to graduate from high school.

The brand gradually disappeared. Jay enrolled in night class, started taking care of business in his day classes and attended all of his mentoring commitments. He stopped drinking and using drugs. He was now on the right track, and his life was changing.

Months down the road, Jay came to one of the mentoring group sessions. Michelle says that, with a backpack in hand, he began to speak. "You all know where and how my life was over the years. I would come to group and not participate or speak up. The reason I opted not to speak was I would have been talking what I was not walking. Today I want to show you all something." Reaching into his backpack, he proudly and confidently pulled out his cap and gown as well as a high school diploma with his name on it, and he placed them on the table in the sight of all in the room. Immediately his peers stood on their feet and began applauding him. According to Michelle, she and all the mentors present were reaching for tissues to wipe the tears off their faces. Jay then began to tell his peers they could accomplish their goals just as he had.

Though not all of the stories of At Promise have the same happy conclusion, the point made is unequivocally clear: mentoring relationships can and will make a difference in the lives of the fatherless.

Biblical Starting Point

The community of faith has always played an important role in fathering the fatherless. In the Old Testament, provision for the fatherless was woven into the context of the law; in the New Testament, God once again places the responsibility on the community. James articulated the expectation clearly: "Religion that God our Father accepts as pure and faultless is this: to look after orphans and widows in their distress and to keep oneself from being polluted by the world" (Jas 1:27).

One aspect of a community's proof of religion or its relationship with God is its response to orphans. It's not enough to be sentimentally sorry; action is required to help alleviate some of the suffering a young person experiences due to the absence of parents—primarily a father. This care of orphans—including those in one-parent homes—is an expectation and responsibility assigned to the community of faith.

Fatherhood was also to be modeled and mentored by leaders within the Christian community. In 1 Timothy 3:1-5 and Titus 1:5-8, the characteristics of a leader are defined. They include the ability to refrain from corruption and vices, such as heavy drinking and violence. Also leaders were to have the ability to manage their own households lovingly and well. The rationale is that if they can't take care of their own families, how can they take care of God's family? While the verses don't directly address fathering, good leadership is hallmarked by healthy relationships and by fulfilling responsibilities in the home.

Mentoring can be a way to provide fathering for the many children who lack a father's presence. Probably the most well-known example is that of Paul and Timothy. While Paul wasn't Timothy's biological father, he was his spiritual father in the faith (1 Cor 4:16-17; 1 Tim 1:18-19; 2 Tim 2:1). As a spiritual father, Paul mentored Timothy by wholeheartedly following Christ, by teaching Timothy what God had taught him, by praying for him and encouraging him through his struggles. For Paul, mentoring wasn't one-dimensional but symbiotic. Paul's life was enriched by Timothy's life as well. At times Paul expressed a need for Timothy—as much as Timothy had a need for Paul (Rom 16:21; 1 Cor 4:17; 2 Tim 4:21).

Leighton Ford defines mentoring as "a relational experience in which one person (mentor) empowers another (mentee) by sharing God-given resources."[1] Throughout Scripture are numerous examples of mentoring. Elijah and Elisha are a familiar example from the Old Testament. In the context of that mentoring relationship, we have Elisha's famous request for a double portion of Elijah's spirit. He had to spend time with the older prophet and follow him closely enough to receive the divine empowerment that he so desperately wanted and needed (2 Kings 2:9-13).

In the New Testament, Priscilla and Aquila mentored Apollos and led him into a deeper and fuller relationship with God (Acts 18:24-26). Paul referred to Timothy as his son in the faith and empowered Timothy's life and ministry through his lifestyle, his teaching, his prayers and his encouragement (1 Tim 1:2, 18; 6:20).

Jesus, however, is the prime example of a mentor. He took twelve disciples and gave them everything he had to empower them to do the Father's will. He shared with his disciples the resources of his word, of his Spirit and of his very life. Through the mentoring experience, his mentees became something they would not have otherwise been.

The Benefits of Mentoring

Mentoring benefits the lives of the children and young adults in many ways.

Mentoring aids in the mentee's character formation. The mentor has an opportunity to explore the mentee's strengths and weaknesses. When these areas are discovered, the mentor can help the person grow and mature by affirming those strengths and helping the mentee to develop in areas of weakness. For example, some of the fatherless young men I've mentored in our church struggled with having a good work ethic. One week they have a job, the next week they quit because they're tired or simply don't feel like going to work.

One young man would get sick every time he got a job. This went on for a couple of years. Finally, after many conversations, times of prayer, accountability sessions and a number of straight-forward reprimands, Bob turned a corner. He has currently been working the same job for over a year. He feels great about the accomplishment, and so do I. When he sees me, he holds his head high and says, "Pastor, I've got a year under my belt." The reality is, he has more than a year under his belt. He has learned the value of discipline and commitment, and he is now in the place to share with another young person or child what he has learned about the value of honest work.

Mentoring helps mentees to set and accomplish goals. Another fatherless young man whom I have mentored for several years dreamed of completing his education. We sat down and talked about his dream, and we mapped out a plan of action. Today he is fulfilling his dream, and I have the privilege of watching him achieve it and of providing support and encouragement to him along the way.

Mentoring grows the mentor. Mentors discover that those they pour time and energy into pour back into their life as well. Each of the young men I've mentored has added something positive to my life. For example, if I challenge them concerning their work ethic, I'm forced to look at my own. I have to make sure I practice what I preach. The young man I encouraged to fulfill his dream of going to school was one of my greatest sources of encouragement during my doctoral work. He constantly told me I could do it and to hang in there. A reciprocal process can occur: the mentor benefits as much as the mentee.

Mentoring requires that the mentor give of her or his resources to the mentee. The mentor takes the things learned in life, such as knowledge, wisdom and experience, and freely gives them to the mentee. The mentor makes a personal investment from the vaults of his or her own substance into the life of the mentee. It's this investment that empowers. To empower the mentee, the mentor must be a good listener and questioner. I believe that to affect someone's heart, you have to listen to her or his heart. Listening and asking good questions aids in the process.

Empowering requires that the mentor be intentional about the process and create a plan for where he or she wants to go. It's more than just taking the mentee out for an occasional Coke. The mentor spends time with the mentee to help that person develop individual strengths and overcome weaknesses. For this to occur, a deliberate strategy is needed. In Bob's case, our plan was to make sure he was out looking for a job. When we met, he had to report on his progress. If he failed to fulfill his obligation, I asked why. When he landed the job, we discussed the fact that he needed to stay at the job for a year, regardless of the pay. The money wasn't the issue; his character was.

Developing a plan of action was a big help to Bob, and it's important that you have a plan of action with the person you mentor. The plan should be developed as a joint venture. A good mentor spends adequate time with the mentee and serves that individual in the Spirit of Christ with love and with prayers, by being transparent and by having a willingness to receive as well as give. The mentee must have a spirit to learn and receive from the mentor. The mentee must be open and honest, and willing to commit to the mentoring relationship.

E. J. is his name, and as long as I can remember, he has been a mentor and father to fatherless young men. Since 1980 he has been a father to approximately ninety boys. His inauguration in this ministry came about through his pastor, Sam Johnson. A boy came to the church whose mother was strung out on drugs. In a quandary over what to do, Pastor Sam enlisted E. J. and the rest is history.

E. J. says, "I'm the only father that many of these boys will ever know." When some of these boys make it to E. J.'s doorstep, they're broken and abused. He takes them in and gives them large doses of love, encouragement, direction and accountability. He says, "Many of these boys have no idea of what a man should be. They are in need of seeing a model of a godly man before them." E. J. says it's a twenty-four-hour-a-day job.

One thing he does is speak positive messages into the boys' lives. Even when they fail, he keeps telling them they will succeed. Another activity that E. J. deems as essential is prayer. He says it takes a lot of prayer. Also, these boys are taught the Word of God and are brought to the house of God faithfully. While some of the boys haven't continued down the right path, many of them are serving God, going to high school, raising families, finishing college and doing great.

Children and young men and women who desperately need a father's input abound in our churches. The church has a great opportunity to impact children and youths through mentoring from birth through their late twenties. A harsh reality exists: if the church will not mentor these children, the streets will. The good news is that we don't have to allow the streets or any other negative force to mentor our children. We can do it! Through the vehicle of mentoring, the church has the opportunity to help people rise above their misfortunes and become the people God intends them to be.

Mobilizing Your Church

Here are several ways your church can be mobilized to mentor the fatherless.

Teach and preach on the subject of mentoring. Topics such as servanthood, leadership, discipleship, empowering others and the joy of giving can help to build a foundation in the church for mentoring. The more you equip the people, the better they will be able to do the work of the ministry. You could preach several messages on "Jesus the Discipler," and place the series in a workbook form. Then you would have your own resource to train your task force, and your task force would have a tool to train and equip potential mentors in the future. If you have small groups in your church, make mentoring a lesson topic for a quarter. If you prefer to use materials other than your own, there are a number of good resources to help you equip your task force to equip others to be mentors.

Set an example. The congregation can be encouraged to follow your lead as a pastor. Be realistic—you can't mentor every needy person in your congregation. However, you can take the time to mentor one or two. As you mentor a couple of people, you will provide a good example for others to follow.

Have a simple strategy for mentoring. For example,

- *Identify a person who needs mentoring.* Consider creating a task force of a group of people who could serve as the match-makers, the ones who will match mentors with mentees within the congregation. Or just keep your eyes open and ask God to place a person in your life to mentor.

- *Gather information.* Learn about the person you're mentoring. Ask questions about his or her life. Find out what her or his ambitions and spiritual passions are. Discover his or her likes and dislikes. Find out what she or he hopes to glean from the mentoring relationship. Share about yourself as well.

- *Invent a game plan.* What will the duration of the mentoring relationship be and on what level will it occur? Will it be short term or lifelong, passive or intense? Set up your meeting times and develop a plan of action for the goals you and your mentee hope to accomplish.

- *Invest.* Pour into the life of your mentee from the vaults of your own life. Give him or her anything you have to enrich his or her life for the cause of Christ.

- *Intercede in prayer.* Pray *for* the person you're mentoring and pray *with* the person you're mentoring. Prayer is essential for spiritual growth and development. The mentoring process will be greatly aided through prayer.

This process is simple and provides people with enough structure to mentor someone adequately.

It's important to remember that mentoring centers on relationship. Good relationships require trust, accountability, love, commitment and a willingness to give time. While there are many technical aspects to mentoring, the relational components are all important. If people know that you genuinely love them and are concerned for their well-being, you will have a great opportunity to affect their life deeply for the sake of Christ.

Ease the mind of willing mentors in the congregation from the pressure of having everything figured out at the outset. Encourage them simply to get involved in the lives of those in need. They can learn as they go. The little morsel they feel they have to give through the context of a mentoring relationship can provide a feast for a father-starved child or young adult. Just taking the time to be with a person can have a great impact.

For those desiring a more programmatic approach to mentoring, let's look at a couple of excellent programs.

The Mentoring Project

When New York Times best-selling author and speaker Donald Miller (*Blue Like Jazz, Father Fiction* and more) began the non-profit The Mentoring Project (TMP) several years ago, his heart was to address fatherlessness in America. The purpose of TMP is to inspire and equip faith communities to build sustainable mentoring communities that reach out to those growing up without a father.

TMP recruits and trains mentors. To do this, they offer faith-based training that serves as the foundation for mentoring relationships. Mentors are trained, equipped and sustained so that they can love, model and coach youth in their community, just as Christ did to his disciples and others.

Through the work of an appointed contact person, TMP helps faith communities prayerfully consider mentoring. They have found the faith community to be an essential piece in the development of mentoring, because mentoring done both in community and individually—as opposed to simply mentoring one-on-one—can create a longer-lasting relationship between the mentor and the mentee.

Once trained through TMP, mentors meet with representatives from a matching agency to further their training, as well as to start a relationship with their future mentee. The age of the youth to be mentored generally ranges from seven to fourteen (sometimes up to sixteen). The matching process takes about four to six weeks, depend on the specifics of the mentor/mentee relationship. This process includes a criminal background, DMV and reference check, as well as an in-depth interview process with the mentor, mentee and a legal guardian of the mentee.

Once the matching process is complete, each mentor is expected to spend one hour per week with their mentee. No more than that is expected, but more time than that is definitely encouraged. When and how that time fits into the mentor's and mentee's schedules is up to the mentor. The mentors and mentees also become fully immersed in group activities every other month, which are planned by the contact person. TMP also provides information on organization-wide mentor/mentee events. Throughout the mentoring experience, TMP provides the mentor with support, guidance and counsel.

11:45

In May of 2011, the mayor of our city called a meeting with local pastors to discuss the increase of violence in our neighborhoods. Following the discussion, a group of pastors from various churches and denominations gathered in prayer and devised a strategy called 11:45. 11:45 means each volunteer commits to serving one day—for forty-five minutes—for one year. The goal of 11:45 is to mobilize hundreds people from churches in the Portland area to participate in one of four areas of service to minister to disenfranchised youth. The dimensions of what is called our Presence Strategy are

- *There*—To mobilize groups of people to walk and be a *visible presence* of God's love in troubled hotspots in the city.
- *Share*—To mobilize people to mentor fatherless—and in some cases motherless—children in our community, providing a *connecting presence.*
- *Care*—To mobilize people to provide care for hurting families, including food for violence-affected families, counseling services and pastoral support to those in need. This provides a *loving presence.*
- *Prayer*—To mobilize a team of people to pray specifically for the youth in our community. This is an *interceding presence.*

Originally the goal of 11:45 was to mobilize one hundred volunteers. Three months into the launching of 11:45, over four hundred have committed, and the list continues to grow. We have several teams dressed in lime-green shirts, walking faithfully during the week in troubled areas in our city.

One of the mentoring agencies we collaborate with is Big Brother Big Sister. On the night we conducted our first push, the response was overwhelming. The representative said her branch had never had so many people volunteer at one time. She was blown away, and overjoyed. People are praying, and families are receiving loving care.

The outreach has had great support from the city as well. The mayor's office has been extremely helpful. It has granted 11:45 all the support it needs. The police department has provided training for our volunteers on the violence issue. The city and the police department support and attend all our rallies, and they both contributed to purchase our green T-shirts. The collaboration of the city, county and law enforcement has been very effective and has been key to 11:45's success.

Currently, we are working on another phase of 11:45 in conjunction with the district attorney's office to help youth who have been arrested on misdemeanor crimes. These youth will be court-mandated to spend time with designated pastors. This will give pastors the opportunity to touch the lives of many fatherless youth.

11:45 fits into the mentoring scheme for fatherlessness because statistics tell us that 85 percent of all youth in the penal system come from fatherless homes. It's a collaborative way churches and a community can work together to mentor the fatherless.

Life Changers

Life Changers is a nine-month program designed to mentor believers in helping deepen their lives in the areas of discipleship and ministry, for the purpose of building the church and extending the kingdom of God. The components of the program are

- *Mentoring*—hands-on discipleship by mature seasoned leaders
- *Teaching*—biblical instruction on essential aspects of life and ministry
- *Accountability*—holding mentees accountable to a lifestyle according to biblical standards

- *Service*—emphasizing the importance of servanthood to Christ, the church and the world

- *Growth and development*—encouraging participants to grow into the person Christ has called them to be

- *Ministry*—providing opportunities for ministry inside and outside the walls of the church

Each year the program enrolls a handful of life changers of diverse racial backgrounds. Some of the participants have had a good father experience, but there are always a few who haven't. Pastor Andrew Miller, who leads the program, is up close and hands on in all the lives of the life changers. In many cases, he acts just as if he were their dad. That's probably why some call him "Father Abraham."

Last year, when it was my turn to share with the group, I talked on authority. While I was speaking, two young men in the group were becoming visibly agitated. I knew what was going on; they both had deep father wounds, and they weren't appreciating the content of the discussion. Since I have a good relationship with both of these young men, I stopped and asked them what the problem was. While everyone else sat in silence, the two of them began to gush out why they struggle with authority. The underlying cause of their agitation and hurt is wounds induced by neglectful fathers.

The church community has a biblical mandate to father the fatherless. Mentoring is a vehicle that facilities surrogate fathering, whatever your preference may be. If your desire is to start by implementing an established program or if you want to take a more relaxed, less structured approach, "run the play and get in the game," as my old football coach used to say. You can do this, your church can do this, your ministry or organization can do this. You will find that the rewards you receive from mentoring far outweigh the efforts you put in.

7

PRAYING FOR THE CHILDREN

Though his words were conveying the brokenness of his heart, the anguish we saw on his face spoke deeper and louder than his mouth could express.

Hue sat in our Bible study group, a small, diverse group of people—young and old, black and white, male and female. He shared with us how his son, Curt, had turned his back on Christ and was in an unswerving pursuit of a false religion. Despite his godly upbringing and heritage, there was nothing Hue or anyone else could say or do to sway him from his chosen course. Curt's decisions and actions were breaking his father's heart. With glazed-over eyes from the tears he was fighting to hold back, Hue asked the group to join along in praying for his son.

Without a doubt, Hue had prayed for his son countless times in the past. Now, however, he recognized the need for not only his prayers alone, but also the prayers of others in order to influence his son's life. Truthfully and forcefully stated, "A child needs not only their father's presence, but his prayers too."

A Father's Prayers

Millions of children in our nation and throughout the world live without the benefit of a father's prayers. From a biblical perspective, the father's spiritual influence on a child's life is equally as important as shelter, clothing and a weekly ration of milk and cookies. Fathers are to provide for their child's physical and spiritual needs. In a roundabout way, the ritual of circumcision illustrates a father's responsibility to influence his child spiritually.

Circumcision is a ritual that held powerful father-son relationship implications in the Old Testament. Unlike the firstborn rites, circumcision was performed not simply on the firstborn son, but on every son. Circumcision was conducted at infancy, and it was a private affair between a father, his son and God (Gen 24:2; Lev 12:30). The father was required to start preparing the child for adulthood while he was still an infant.

The father has the opportunity and responsibility to influence his child from infancy to adulthood. Though I strain the interpretation of the rite in saying the following, the implication is still powerful. Specifically, beginning at his son's infancy, the father is required to place a theological mark on his child that will last a lifetime. The father commits to guiding his son into adulthood.

Fathers today need to mark their children's lives for God. In a world where negative and evil forces constantly seek to influence children in wrong directions, a father has the opportunity, in the privacy of his relationship with his child and God, to mark the child's life with a biblical worldview and values. Fathers today must take advantage of the opportunity and fulfill their God-given responsibility to their children. If fathers fail to mark their children, other influences will.

One of the ways a father can place a lasting theological mark on his boy or girl is through the power of prayer. The ability to focus and concentrate intercession to impact a child's life can't be overstated. Prayer releases the power, aid and grace of God to work in a person's life. E. M. Bounds stated, "Prayer has all the force of God in it."[1] Due to the magnitude and enormity of the problems surrounding father absenteeism, a force greater than ourselves is needed to minister to affected individuals. Prayer connects us to that force—God!

God Prays for His Kids

A beautiful truth and reality exists. God our heavenly Father is engaged in a prayer meeting for his children. God is interceding for us! Let's consider two passages that show this.

> The Spirit helps us in our weakness. We do not know what we ought to pray for, but the Spirit himself intercedes for us with groans that words cannot express. And he who searches our hearts knows the mind of the Spirit, because the Spirit intercedes for the saints in accordance with God's will. (Rom 8:26-27)
>
> Now there have been many of those priests, since death prevented them from continuing in office; but because Jesus lives forever, he has a permanent priesthood. Therefore he is able to save completely those who come to God through him, because he always lives to intercede for them. (Heb 7:23-25)

In the Romans passage, we learn that the Holy Spirit prays for God's children. His prayers are based on perfect knowledge of the child and on God's will. Therefore, the Spirit prays perfectly and effectively. His prayers bridge the chasm between the child's weaknesses and God's strength. The result of the prayer is that the child of God is empowered to fulfill God's purpose and plan.

The Hebrews passage states that Jesus always lives to intercede to the Father on behalf of his children. This helps us to understand two important aspects of a child's need for prayer. First, as children grow, develop and encounter trials, temptations, difficulties and transitions, they always stand in need of prayer. The fact that Jesus always lives to intercede for us makes that clear. Second, we all need divine intercession to aid us in becoming the people God intends us to be. While the physical touch of a father is critical to a child's formation, the divine touch from God the Father is more necessary. God himself is interceding to ensure his touch occurs in his children's life.

The question to be asked here is, if God is praying for his children, how much more do we need to be praying for children who have no present earthly father to intercede on their behalf? Our answer to the question: a lot! Every fatherless individual in your sphere of influence needs prayer. Let's discuss some practical ways you can make that happen.

Add Another Gem

In the Old Testament, part of Aaron's priestly garb was the breastpiece. It was a nine-by-nine, artistically crafted, rectangular item worn over Aaron's heart. On the breastpiece were four rows of three gemstones set in gold filigree. Engraved in each of the twelve stones was the name of one of the sons of Israel (Ex 28:15-21). The beauty of this imagery is that Aaron carried the children of Israel on his heart as he came into the presence of God (28:29-30). Whenever he went into the holy of holies, the sons of Israel went in with him.

I'm not only a pastor, but a daddy too. Consistently and daily, when I spend time in prayer before God, my kids' names and needs cross my mind and my heart. I can honestly say I pray for my children almost every day. God hears me beseeching his blessing and grace for Micah, Michelle, McKenzie and Myles. Like Aaron, I bear the gemstones inlaid with gold on my heart, bearing the names of my kids. If you're a parent, I'd venture to say this rings true for you; your kids are engraved on your heart, and you faithfully pray for them.

But let's turn the page. There is a long waiting list of fatherless children waiting to reside on a caring and faithful heart. They are waiting to be treasured as gems, waiting to be valued, waiting to be kept close to some heart, waiting to be prayed for.

God is a father who enlarges not only our territory but also our hearts. God has the ability to broaden the capacity of your heart so he can add another gem (child) to your breastpiece. Bobby or Sandra, whom no one carries on the heart, can lovingly be embedded on your breastpiece, the breastpiece of your church or the breastpiece of your ministry or organization.

Paul and Timothy's relationship gives a vivid picture of a gem being inlaid on the heart of another. The Bible tells us that the matriarchs of Timothy's family heavily influenced him. Timothy's mother and grandmother lived a life of pure and loving devotion to God. Their influence was significant in the formation of Timothy's own journey of faith. The authentic faith modeled and taught by his mom and grandma now was embraced by his own soul. The unfeigned faith that was in them now lived in him. Scripture gives very little information about Timothy's father, except that he was a Greek. There is no indication that his father influenced his spiritual destiny in any shape or fashion. Without a doubt, we know the matriarchs of his family upheld him in prayer, but the father likely made no prayerful contribution. Enter Paul. The following passage shows the place Timothy had in Paul's heart.

> Paul, an apostle of Christ Jesus by the will of God, according to the promise of life that is in Christ Jesus, *To Timothy, my dear son:* Grace, mercy and peace from God the Father and Christ Jesus our Lord. I thank God, whom I serve, as my forefathers did, with a clear conscience, *as night and day I constantly remember you in my prayers.* Recalling your tears, I long to see you, so that I may be filled with joy. I have been reminded of your sincere faith, which first lived in your grandmother Lois and in your mother Eunice and, I am persuaded, now lives in you also. (2 Tim 1:1-5, emphasis added)

Timothy was a gem on Paul's heart. Though he wasn't Paul's

biological son, Paul unashamedly called him his own dear son. Paul not only embraced him as his son, but also prayed for him day and night. By Paul's own admission, Timothy was constantly remembered in his prayers. Like the breastpiece on Aaron heart, bearing the names of the sons of Israel, Paul's heart bore Timothy in love, faithfulness and prayer.

Begin praying for the fatherless by asking your heavenly Father to add another gem on your heart. An admonition of Jesus comes to mind: "Watch and pray." When asking God to enlarge your heart, you're not only praying but watching as well. Pray for the expansion of your heart, but also keep your heart and eyes open for the child God may want to set in your heart. Look down your street. Glance through the congregation. Observe the lonely kid on the sports team. Be certain of this: if you watch and pray, God will place the right child or young adult on your heart. The prayers you pray for that individual will eternally and powerfully affect her or his life. If you watch and pray, God will indeed add another gem to your breastpiece.

Your Personal Prayer Time

One of my relatives kept the cleanest house I've ever seen, but one room in the house was a place that only brave souls dared to tread. That room belonged to the man of the house. It was his territory and his private domain. Any wise souls knew not to approach that door without a mop, broom or other cleaning apparatus. Occasionally, he would ask me to go into the room to retrieve an item. My IQ is not at the top of the chart, but I had undertaken this mission several times in the past. I was keenly aware of the fact that I needed a machete to clear a pathway through the clutter. Otherwise I might vanish in the brush of books, paper, relics and Lord knows what else.

As a pastor or ministry leader, your prayer time may be a little like my relative's room. I know mine is at times. So many needs and priorities clutter your mind and heart. When you go before God in prayer, it's like wading through a room of clutter, and at times you just want to run out, screaming. Now here I am, asking you to add another burden to your prayer time. We know that, though at times we have to dredge through the mounds of burdens, cares and woes, the place of prayer is the place of survival. The words of the old hymn are true: our daily time with God is the sweet hour of prayer that draws us from a world of care. Therefore, despite the clutter, we do pray so that God can bring order and blessing to the sometimes chaotic situations we face.

Like Paul, who travailed for Christ to be formed in the lives of the Christians in Galatia (Gal 4:19), you have the privilege of travailing for the fatherless in your congregation. Your prayers will work to form wonderful changes in the lives of those affected by the repercussions of father absenteeism. Here are a few suggestions you can use to incorporate consistent prayer for the fatherless into your private prayer time.

- *Create a prayer list.* Write the names of individuals affected by fatherlessness in your church, ministry or organization, and during your prayer time pray over their names.

- *Identify a specific time slot.* Determine to set aside an allotted amount of time to pray for individuals affected by fatherlessness. Set a specific time during the day, or make the commitment to pray several times throughout the day.

- *Contact and pray.* Sometimes I have a conversation with a person who is affected by fatherlessness, and then I pray privately about things we discussed in our conversation.

- *Pray for those in crisis.* I'm sure in your church, organization or ministry you hear reports of individuals in crisis and trouble. Use that information as ammunition for prayer.

- *Pray for workers.* Ask God to raise up people in your church, ministry or organization who have a burden and heart to work with the fatherless.

James encourages us, saying, "The prayer of a righteous [person] is powerful and effective" (5:16). By incorporating intercession for the fatherless into your prayer time, your prayers will make a powerful difference for those in your sphere of influence who are impacted by fatherlessness.

Corporate Prayer

Prayer with others is also important. Hue prayed individually for his son, but he also solicited the prayer of other believers. In the book of Acts, several accounts of the force of corporate prayer are illustrated. One example is found in Acts 4. Peter and John were jailed for speaking in the name of Christ. When they were released from jail, they were threatened and ordered not to speak in the name of Jesus anymore. And their first order of business was to communicate to the community of faith what had just transpired.

The community's response to the immediate crisis was prayer. The Scripture says, "They raised their voices together in prayer to God" (Acts 4:24). The community engaged in corporate prayer, and God answered in a miraculous fashion. The place where they were praying was shaken, and they were all filled with a supernatural boldness. God also worked miracles to meet the needs of hurting people and to strengthen the community in its ministry task.

I believe if the church will corporately pray for fatherless children, single moms and broken fathers, God will work. Just as in the account in Acts, God will work miracles in the lives of the people for whom we pray, and he will continue to give our congregations the wisdom and strength they need to minister to the fatherless. So then, how does a pastor or a leader mobilize the congregation to pray for the fatherless?

Small groups or existing prayer groups. Small, intimate settings can provide a powerful opportunity for prayer. The size of the group allows members to harness their hearts around persons in your church, ministry or organization who struggle with fatherlessness.

Your current times of corporate prayer. The pastoral prayer on Sunday mornings could be a time when the congregation is encouraged to pray for the fatherless. If your church has regularly scheduled prayer times, intercession prayer for the fatherless can be injected.

A prayer card. Create a simple card with a couple of Scripture passages on it pertaining to ministry to the fatherless. Place on it the names of families in the church who have father needs. Also pray for marriages or whatever else pertains to the issue. Be creative and design the card to fit the needs of your particular congregation. Make sure everyone receives a card, and encourage the people to pray using their prayer card.

Concerts of prayer. The concert of prayer is a concept often used to pray for missions. It involves taking a designated period and dividing it into individual segments with specific emphasis given to smaller aspects of a bigger picture. You could have a concert of prayer at your church to pray for the fatherless. For example, once or twice a year, designate one of your evening services or small-group times as a concert of prayer for them.

The prayer time could last only an hour. Divide it into six ten-minute segments. Give each segment a different emphasis. One segment may be to pray for children whose fathers are absent. Another could be to pray for strength and aid for single mothers, and another could be to pray for marriages. For each segment, have different people lead the prayer and focus time. They would simply share a passage and encourage the congregation to pray together for a few minutes on that particular focus point. I suggest that a concert of prayer be the job of a task force. Allow them to plan and facilitate the entire process.

Altar calls. At times I invite individuals who are struggling in this area to come to the altar for prayer. They come, and our prayer

FATHERLESS PRAYER GUIDE

Pray for fatherless individuals

- To experience the validation they need, that they would know they are valuable and they matter
- To experience healing from the pain of rejection and from the anger, shame, hurt and disillusionment that accompany the wound
- For good role models and surrogate fathers to enter their lives
- For the resources they need to grow, develop and become the person God intends them to be
- For God to fill the fatherless void in their heart and life
- Freedom from the addictions, criminal behavior, promiscuity and other harmful avenues they may have taken to fill the fatherless void
- For the fatherless to know and embrace God as their heavenly Father

Pray for people serving the fatherless

- For single mothers to have the wisdom, strength and support to effectively raise their children in a fatherless environment
- For compassion and wisdom for those who are working in mentoring roles with the fatherless
- For churches, organizations and ministries to be encouraged and to grow in their efforts to combat fatherlessness
- For God to use your life to make a difference in the life of the fatherless

Pray for prevention

- For healthy marriages
- For men to assume their responsibilities as fathers and to be taught how to be good fathers
- For biblical strategies to prevent teen and out-of-wedlock pregnancies
- For families and traditional family structures to be strengthened
- For men and women to allow Christ to be Lord of their lives

Permission to reproduce this prayer guide is granted as long as no fee is charged.

Taken from *Church for the Fatherless* by Mark E. Strong, © 2012, and used by permission of InterVarsity Press <www.ivpress.com>.

Figure 2

team prays for them. It's amazing the comfort and strength an individual can receive during special times in the presence of God.

What to Pray For

One of the challenges of praying for the fatherless problem is knowing what exactly to pray for. While each person has unique experiences, needs and struggles, there are some general points that can guide you. Prayer for the fatherless should encompass three key areas:

1. Prayer needs to be offered for affected individuals.

2. Prayer is necessary for people whom God will use to minister to the needs of the fatherless.

3. Prayers should be offered to prevent fatherlessness from occurring.

The Fatherless Prayer Guide in figure 2 covers these core areas. This list can serve as a guide to help you, your church, your ministry or your organization pray for the fatherless.

A Testimony to the Power of Prayer

Amy is one of the fatherless. She and her siblings were raised in a well-to-do community. They were educated in good schools, dressed in nice clothes and taught good manners. Unfortunately, the façade masked an inward nightmare.

She had a father in her home, but her experience of him from the time she was very young was of a man who hurt, scared and confused her, rather than being a father. Sexually, physically and mentally abused over many years, Amy has struggled to live a "normal" life. Her father's actions affected her mind and body, and often her ability to function.

Amy became a Christian in her early thirties. A few months later, she attended a Christian women's conference where she had an intense experience. As she and the other women were worshiping God, she felt a sudden bolt of light from above knock her to the floor. She began to cry out, and she asked those who came to her if she was dying. Four women surrounded her, assured her she wasn't dying and began to pray intensely for her. When she stood up, she felt completely empty. The women came to her side again and stayed with her until she was immersed in the Holy Spirit.

Amy describes this baptism and experience with Christ as the main beginning of her healing. She says, "It was my experience of a totally alive Jesus who loved me and who touched my mind with his loving hands that changed my life." Shortly after that experience, she realized more clearly what her father had done to her, and she began to take steps to get healed.

In the first few years of her healing, Amy found help not only from her church and Bible teaching, but also from counselors, books, medications and a hospital program for survivors of severe abuse. While all of those helped her, she acknowledges two things that impacted her healing and survival: "It has been God who has saved my life and has helped me heal in so many ways. And I feel that he chose to have some of my healing happen through the prayers of others. I don't know why, but I know that his thoughts are not our thoughts and I know that he heals different people in different ways." She continues,

> Prayer is powerful. Very powerful. And God seems to have used certain people to pray for me intensely at different times. I don't understand why it has worked this way, but in my experience God has used people who have a heart to pray with fervor. There have been so many times over the last twenty-plus years when I didn't know what else to do but to ask people to pray for me.
>
> Many times I couldn't even describe what the problem was. Sometimes I could; at those times I would describe to

the prayer warrior "I'm losing interest in staying here (on earth) and it's scaring me," or "I can't think clearly, but I don't want to take any medications to 'fix it,'" or "I'm having bad flashbacks/dreams of what happened to me, and it's awful." Especially in the last few years, I wait to ask someone to pray for me only when I feel I have totally exhausted all other ways to get out of pain and it isn't getting any better. Time and time again, within a few hours of the person(s) praying, I get major relief and am able to function again.

Why do I need all this prayer by others? Why can't just my own prayers take care of the problem? Why can't I "just get quickly totally healed" from my hurts? And what could have hurt me so badly that I'm still affected by it all these years later?

You know, I don't really know the answers to those questions. As I get older, I no longer am tormented by those questions. I think they are more the questions of those who get frustrated that I'm still having major struggles at times. One pastor even told me that they are baffled why I'm not "further along by now" in my Christian walk. I understand their frustration with me. I don't expect them to understand if they haven't experienced severe abuse. But I also understand the silence and the haunted look of others who have been through things like me.

For those of us who had fathers, but they abused us, it's often very hard to talk about it. It's hard to describe it, and it's hard to figure out "what is wrong with me/us" as the abuse can affect so many parts of our body, soul and mind. I hope that those in ministry will be able to see the value of praying for the fatherless and that, in some cases, it will be their compassionate prayers that lead to deeper healing.

Amy's story clearly lets us know the power of prayer and why we should pray for the fatherless. In the familiar words we've heard countless times in our places of worship, "Let us now bow our heads for a word of prayer." I'd like to add another stroke to that request. Let us not only bow our heads, but "now let us bow our hearts as well in prayer for the fatherless." Let us be confident that God's heart is tender toward the fatherless, and he will graciously answer us as we pray.

Let us pray.

GOD OUR FATHER

Jamie's Story

Jamie is a young Caucasian woman in our church in whose life God has done a beautiful work of transformation. I will never forget the first time she came into my office. She had on combat boots and a tank top, and had tattoos and a few piercings. I had no clue what was on her mind or what she wanted to talk about. As we began to talk, she told me of changes that were starting to take place in her life that she didn't understand. She explained how her desires were changing and how she felt love that she had never experienced before. Part of Jamie's struggle with God was the poor relationship she'd had with her father.

Her relationship with her father muted her to the possibility that anyone or anything associated with men or a father was any good—even God. Here's her story:

> I did not have a good relationship with my biological father or with men in general during my childhood and up to about thirty years old. The idea of a father was an unsafe concept to me. I can remember countless times where my dad put the

lives of me and my siblings in jeopardy due to his drinking. The idea of a heavenly Father or God was also a foreign concept to me and was never discussed in my household.

When I first started asking questions about God, my mom couldn't answer me. Being from Utah, most of my friends were LDS [Later-Day Saints], and they would say that our heavenly Father protects us, but if I didn't get baptized, then I was going to hell. After being told that so many times, I pretty much dismissed the idea of God, because no supreme being would be so mean. At the same time I gave up trying to love my dad or count on him in times of need. Every year at my birthday, when I didn't get a phone call or holidays would go by without him showing any interest, the idea that dads didn't matter was cemented into my being.

My heart was hardened against my dad, men and my heavenly Father. Every aspect of my outward life showed others that I didn't need a man or God. I became more like a man to avoid or scare other men. I chose to be in a relationship with another woman for almost ten years to prove outwardly that I could make it without being supported by any man. And I became very outwardly "informed" about atheism. But it was all a façade. That life *never* felt right in my heart. I went further and further away from God to avoid being hurt . . . which now makes no sense at all.

God never left me; Jesus saved me, and at the right time, he started to give me understanding about my dad. Through a school project, God showed me the tragedies in my dad's life from an early age. God showed me the disconnections in my dad's family. I learned that me and my dad had a lot in common. I remember calling him and saying, "Dad, I want you to know I forgive you for everything that has happened in the past and I love you."

Since that moment in time, my heart no longer hurts because of the lack of love. Forgiving and loving my dad through Jesus has set me free from the pain. I can say that even if today my dad had decided to move on without me, my heart is no longer hard. There is still work to be done, yet I pray every day to have God's will in my life, because without Jesus, I am lost.

Jamie's story tells us that a biblical perspective on fatherhood is essential. Children need to have a correct picture of God as father. We have a tendency to define God as father by anthropology, culture or our personal experiences with our fathers, as it was with Jamie, instead of through biblical theology. It's easy for us to say God is like this or that based on our experience, cultural values and mores. However, depending on our experience or the dogma of the culture could be detrimental.

The danger of our assumptions is that in some cases the Scriptures may not verify our claims. The Bible allows God to define himself to us as Father through his own Word. Above all, individuals suffering from a fatherless wound need the healing that only our heavenly Father can give.

God the Father in the Old Testament

While it's evident from the Old Testament Scriptures that God is a father who disciplines his children, he is by no means portrayed as a harsh, authoritarian despot. God is a loving, compassionate and caring father. The theme of God being a father of love, compassion and care is woven throughout the tapestry of the Old Testament. Some of the beautiful strands that form this tapestry are interlaced through several key passages (Ps 103:13-14; Is 63:16; 64:8). One such passage is found in Hosea. Referring to God's loving paternal nature, the section reads,

> When Israel was a child, I loved him, and out of Egypt I
> called my son. But the more I called Israel, the further they

went from me. They sacrificed to the Baals and they burned incense to images. It was I who taught Ephraim to walk, taking them by the arms; but they did not realize it was I who healed them. I led them with cords of human kindness, with ties of love; I lifted the yoke from their neck and bent down to feed them. (Hos 11:1-4)

Hosea portrays God not as a strict authoritarian father, but as a father who loves his child. God is the father who taught Israel to live and to walk by lovingly taking them by the hand and guiding them step-by-step. He is the father who healed his people because of his love for them.

In his thesis "The Fatherhood of God," David Wenzel points out that God's love as a parent is also emphasized in the metaphor of a mother's love for her children (footnote 7). Isaiah powerfully communicates the point: "Can a mother forget the baby at her breast and have no compassion on the child she has borne? Though she may forget, I will not forget you! See, I have engraved you on the palms of my hands; your walls are ever before me" (49:15-16).

The mother metaphor expresses God's love by showing that he is the one who gave birth to his son, Israel, through travail and pain and tears (Is 42:14). His motherly love also will not allow him to ever forget the baby on his breast or the child he has borne. Finally, as a mother he provides ongoing comfort for his buffeted child (66:13). Like the father metaphor, the mother metaphor provides powerful insight into the loving, compassionate and merciful parental nature of God. Often care and compassion are viewed solely as female/mother responsibilities. In Scripture we see God modeling fatherhood as tender and compassionate.

God is also a faithful father. The faithfulness of God as a parent is communicated in Psalm 27:10. It is superior to natural parents' in that he never abandons his offspring. When natural parents do abandon their children, God receives them. The Scripture states,

"Though my father and mother forsake me, the LORD will receive me." The faithfulness of God as a father is of no little significance, especially in the light of the father crisis in our culture today. Earthly fathers can and will be unfaithful. Our heavenly Father, however, will always be a constant.

A final attribute of God as father has to do with justice (Ps 9; 16; 84:14; Job 8:3; 34:12; 37:23). Isaiah 30:18 states this attribute succinctly: "Yet the LORD longs to be gracious to you; he rises to show you compassion. For the LORD is a God of justice. Blessed are all who wait for him!"

The Father Revealed by Jesus

There they were, gathered around him at mealtime: Jesus their master, teacher and Lord. For the past three years, the disciples had watched his every move, hung on his every word and marveled at his wonderful workings. However, in the course of one meal, their world began to dissolve. Judas left the dinner table not to better the fellowship, but to destroy it. Peter, one of the insiders in the band, heard that he would do the unthinkable and deny the Master as well.

Then the ultimate bomb was dropped. Jesus told this motley crew that he would be taken from them. The meal that had hours ago started off as a celebration had become a platter of pain and grief. In the midst of the confusion and sorrow, Philip bellowed out a request to ease the collective pain and disappointment of the group: "Lord, show us the father." To which Jesus boldly replies, "Anyone who has seen me has seen the Father" (Jn 14:9).

While God is revealed as a father in the Old Testament, he is even more profoundly revealed as such in the New Testament. Jesus himself is the principal revealer of the Father. In his life and ministry, a portrait of God as father is hung before us.

Much of what Jesus teaches, preaches and models concerning the Father we see through the context of the kingdom of God. God

Almighty is the Father of the kingdom who is concerned for each of his children, not simply on a national level, as seen in the Old Testament. God is also Father on a personal and community level as it relates to the community of faith emerging in Jesus Christ. In his exposé on the kingdom, Jesus articulates several remarkable qualities of our heavenly Father.

In the New Testament, Jesus introduced a new paradigm; his usage of the term "our Father" in his prayers and teaching is quite different from that of the Old Testament. The difference being, in the OT God was portrayed as a father who provides discipline, and is loving and compassionate. In the NT, all the above applies to God as father. However, the NT reveals God as father who is close and personal. He is so close and intimate in our lives that we cry Abba Father. Joachim Jeremias observes that while the community prays to God as father and individuals may speak of God as heavenly Father, "There is as of yet no evidence in the literature of ancient Palestinian Judaism that 'my Father' is used as personal address to God."[1] Concerning early Judaism, Robert Hamerton-Kelly expresses the same sentiments: "Therefore although early Judaism differs from the Old Testament by invoking God as father, this invocation does not indicate a personal intimacy with God, of the kind which is the hallmark of Jesus' use of 'father' in his prayers."[2]

One key word that gives tremendous insight into Jesus' use of *father* is the word *Abba*. In the garden of Gethsemane, Jesus cries out to his Father using the word *Abba*, denoting intimacy between a father and child. The word also implied a trusting and obedient surrender to the will of God on the part of the child. It not only expresses his attitude of obedience and trust (Mk 14:36), but also acknowledges his incomparable authority (Mt 11:25ff).[3]

In Matthew 6:9, Jesus invited his disciples to participate in the same family relationship by instructing them to pray saying, "Our Father." By saying, "our Father," Jesus places the disciples in relationship to him as well as to God. The relationship is to be intimate to the point of asking God to meet our needs, and it requires obedience to forgive as God forgives.

The notion of God as "our Father" has powerful implications in terms of today's fatherhood crisis. God is a universal father, and if children place their trust in him, they have a father who will be intimate with them and present with them.

Ticole's Story

Ticole is a young man who has had a difficult time trusting God to be his father. The reason for the difficulty stems from his experience with a non-present biological father and the presence of a difficult stepfather. Listen.

> My mom had always told me that my father was a policeman. One day a policeman was visiting our house. I was only five, so I enthusiastically asked the man in the blue uniform with the shiny badge, "Are you my daddy?" He responded by telling me, "No, I am not your daddy!" Sadly, he was. When the door closed behind him, my mother said to me, "That was your dad."
>
> Those brief moments I spent with the policeman were tragic for two reasons. One, it was the first time I saw my father, and it was the last time I saw him. I heard he had two other kids, but his presence and influence in my life is nonexistent. The sadder truth was my mom had had an abortion with an earlier child with this man, and he wanted her to abort me as well. In my case, my mom chose different. My mom devoted my life to the Lord to be used for his purposes.
>
> Eventually my mom married. I had no relationship with my biological father, and the relationship with my stepfather was worse. He abused me; he stole from me and devalued me as a person. On one occasion, he was trying to give me a haircut that I didn't need. To accomplish the feat, he busted

my head opened on the sink. Rage and hatred began to fester in my heart toward my fathers and men in general. I started to hate my mother as well. She would constantly allow this man to come back into our house repeatedly after he would abandon her. When he was gone, I was relieved; when he returned, it was hell. I did not feel safe in my home.

I started to act out to get attention. When I was good, I was totally unnoticed. When I acted out, I received attention that I so desperately needed, even though it was for the wrong reasons.

Sometimes I wished that my mother had gone ahead and aborted me. No one ever stood up for me to my stepfather except my grandmother on one occasion. I felt like I was never wanted as a person. What made the situation more difficult was my stepfather made a good effort to be a positive influence in my stepbrother's life, but not mine.

My experiences with the fathers in my life made it extremely difficult, if not impossible, to trust God. I had been let down by all the men in my life, so how could God be any different? My father track record had taught me not to expect anything positive from anyone. I trusted no man, so how could I trust God? I believed God would fail me too.

In spite of my prison of pain, God broke through. At a men's retreat at our church, I asked God the question, Why didn't my father want me. That was the first time I ever verbalized the throbbing question that haunted my life. In the depth of my heart, he let me know in a special way that he wanted me. The other instance took place at the altar of our church when I received prayer for God to help me with my abandonment issues. A weight dropped off my heart that day, and I experienced healing and cleansing.

Still I had a ways to go. It was not until I experienced a failed relationship that God began to tenderize my heart in a way I had never experienced. Out of that experience, I found comfort in God. I learned that God is a good father who can be trusted. He has integrity and character, something I had never seen in the men in my life. God then placed me in a church where I could be around older men of integrity. Now my life is changing. My passion is to be a man of integrity and to know my heavenly Father more. I want to be a role model for younger kids who do not have godly men in their lives.

I trust God and believe him more. The doubts are shrinking, and I feel safe in him. God is bringing peace and healing to things. I am able to look past my earthly father and see my heavenly Father. I know God's Word is true. I was bitter and learned how to love and released the bitterness. I made bad choices in the past, trying to meet needs in my life. Now I have my heavenly Father to meet my needs.

As Ticole learned, the fatherless have a heavenly Father who wants to meet the needs they have in their life. They just need to know it and, like Ticole, learn to trust God to be the Father they so desperately need. He will not fail them; he will take care of every need in their life.

Your Heavenly Father Will Meet Your Needs

In the Sermon on the Mount, Jesus reveals God as a father who provides. Jesus instructs his listeners not to worry about life (Mt 6:25-34). He contends that life constitutes more than our daily necessities. He therefore specifically tells his hearers not to worry about food or clothing. His rationale for the neglect of worry about self-preservation is that the Father in heaven will take care of those needs for you. He reasons that if God takes care of the birds of the air and clothes the flowers of the field, he will take care of his children as well. God will and does take care of his children.

An underlying reality of God as a father is his omniscience.

His ability to know all things functions not only in deep and weighty matters of the universe, but in all things pertaining to the intricate needs of his children. D. A. Carson states, "The personal Father God to whom the believers pray does not require information about our needs. As a father knows the needs of his family, yet teaches them to ask in confidence and trust, so does God treat his children."[4]

As a good father, God knows the needs of his children, and he provides for those needs through prayer (Mt 7:9, 11; Lk 11:13).

God as a loving and merciful father is another theme in the kingdom context. God's mercy and love are shown in his response to his children and in his creation. As a merciful father, God is concerned for his children. He is concerned about their whereabouts, their protection and their overall well-being (Mt 18:10, 12-14; Lk 17:1-2). Mark further illustrates this point.

> People were bringing little children to Jesus to have him touch them, but the disciples rebuked them. When Jesus saw this, he was indignant. He said to them, "Let the little children come to me, and do not hinder them, for the kingdom of God belongs to such as these. I tell you the truth, anyone who will not receive the kingdom of God like a little child will never enter it." And he took the children in his arms, put his hands on them and blessed them. (10:13-16)

God's care and mercy for his little ones are obvious. Scripture teaches that his kingdom consists of people who are childlike, and his concern and attention are directed to his little ones.

God's mercy and love are also seen in his willingness to forgive the sins of his children. God is a forgiving father (Mt 6:12, 14, 15; Mk 11:25; Lk 23:34). One poignant illustration is found in Matthew 18:22-35. In this passage Peter asks the Lord how many times he is required to forgive a person in a given day, to which Jesus replies, basically, "As much as you need to." Jesus goes on to tell a story of a man who was forgiven a debt that he lacked the means to repay. As a result of his appeal for clemency, the merciful king exonerated him from his debt. After the release, the forgiven man found someone who owed him a few cents and viciously demanded payment. The king then revoked his previous ruling toward the man. The story implies that, while God is a forgiving God, he also demands that his children follow suit.

Finally, as a father, God is loving and merciful, both to those who are a part of his kingdom and to those who are not. Jesus said, "But I tell you: Love your enemies and pray for those who persecute you, that you may be sons of your Father in heaven. He causes his sun to rise on the evil and the good, and sends rain on the righteous and the unrighteous" (Mt 5:44-45). The essence of God's love and mercy is seen in the instructions he gives his children to follow. The disciples are instructed to love their enemies and to pray for them. They are to emulate their Father in heaven, who causes the sun to rise on the just and the unjust.

Paul on God the Father

In many of Paul's letters, the father image is central to his doctrine of God. It serves to unite the community of believers as one family. For Paul, God is a father who adopts spiritually orphaned children and gives them all the rights and privileges of legitimate sons and daughters by making them joint heirs with Christ (Rom 8:15-17).

In his discourse to the Galatians, Paul began a discussion on Abraham, the father of Israel. Within the context of the Abrahamic metaphor, Paul reminded the readers of God's promise to Abraham that he would bless his seed (Gal 3:16-18). He then explained that the seed is Christ. The significance is that, through Christ, God has formed his household. Family membership and offspring rites are realized in the Father through the Son (Gal 3:26-29). Like the model Old Testament father, God provides an inheritance for his children because we are all heirs to the promise. We are members of his household.

For Paul, the reality and assurance of our status as adopted children of the Father is culminated in the witness and the work of the Spirit.[5] The Spirit of the Son cries out, "'Abba,' Father" (Rom 8:15-17; Gal 4:4-7). This cry is not based on a heady or purely intellectual response. It is an intimate cry based on the individual experience of faith—the experience whereby God helps believers to know in the depths of their person that he is their father indeed.

Paul also used the designation of *father* for liturgical purposes. Concerning Paul's liturgical usage of God as father, Hamerton-Kelly makes several observations. First, he makes the point that Paul began all his letters with a greeting that designates God as father in relationship to the Lord Jesus Christ. The greeting "Grace and peace from God the Father and the Lord Jesus Christ" is used in a number of passages (for example, Rom 1:7; 1 Cor 1:3; 2 Cor 1:2; Gal 1:3).

Second, Hamerton-Kelly stresses the point that the same formula is used in the giving of thanks (1 Thess 1:2-3), in the making of an oath (2 Cor 11:31), as an acclamation (Phil 2:11), for intercession (1 Thess 3:11-13), as a benediction (Rom 15:6), in a baptismal liturgy (Rom 6:4) and as a creed (1 Cor 8:6; 15:24).[6]

Paul's use of God as father in all these instances conveys a reality that existed in the lives of the early believers on a private and public level. God was a living and real father to them in their experience. He was the one who adopted them and made them heirs through his Son. He was the one who placed in their hearts the cry of the Spirit. He was more to them than just dogma or doctrine; he was their father. Hamerton-Kelly captures this beautifully when he writes, "The early Christians did not talk about God as Father, they talked with him."[7]

Paul stressed that regardless of pedigree, gender or ethnicity, all believers have access to all the blessings and grace provided for them by their heavenly Father. The children are assured of the reality of this relationship by the cry of the Spirit in their hearts that rings out saying, "Abba, Father." The reality of God as father is also communicated in forms of worship, liturgy and prayers.

Children need to live in this reality as well. They need a family to belong to, and they need a father they can call their own. This reality needs to be internal as well as external—just as God the Father assures us internally that we are his and we are a part of his family.

John's Story

John is a young man who has been attending our church for a few years, and he and my son Micah have become close friends. The fact that he feels comfortable sharing his story is evidence in and of itself of God's grace at work in his life. John's story is a great example of how God's family can help a fatherless person know God can be his heavenly Father too.

My dad was around, but we never connected. We never talked, and I felt like I didn't have a father. I was very empty. My dad was abusive, and I got to the point where I didn't even want to call him Dad. In fact, whenever I heard his name, I became angry. My anger, of course, stemmed from the rejection. My dad had even told me that he wanted me to change my last name.

Eventually I went to a foster family; it was a great situation, and everyone loved me. My foster dad was helpful and healthy; but then after four years he passed away. The hurt then resurfaced, and I was back in the same situation again.

I had become walled off and refused to let anyone penetrate my protective shell. I started going to church, and God started to use the church family to help me.

Through our church's Life Changers program, I learned to trust God. We had a small retreat, and I cried for a solid two hours. Mama Cora loved on me and encouraged me to just let it all out. You have to understand, I am not a crybaby, but God gripped my heart. I had never cried that long in my life. God was releasing all the pain I had bottled up for all those years. When I finished crying, I felt God really loved me.

In our church, God has given me more family. I have some good spiritual brothers, aunts, uncles, moms and dads. My life is much more open now. I am free to share with others, where before I was a closed book. I now believe God will use my hardships to help others. They will make me a better man and husband when I get married.

Sometimes things still get hard for me. But I always hear God speak these words to my heart: "I will never leave you or forsake you." When I hear these words spoken to my heart, it always brings a smile to my face. Philemon 7 says, "Your love has given me great joy and encouragement, because you, brother, have refreshed the hearts of the saints." I believe God will use my life to bring great joy and encouragement to others, just as God has used his family to bring healing and encouragement to me.

Help Them See

The Bible teaches us that God is a good father who provides for the needs of his children. Primarily, he is a father who blesses his children in a context of a loving and intimate relationship. That was the case with Jamie, Ticole and John, whose view of God as a father was blurred by their view of their natural father. There are countless other individuals groping in darkness, hampered by blinders attached by bad fathers. They are desperate and hungry for a father, wasting and languishing away inside for the lack thereof.

Pastors and leaders have their jobs cut out for them in this fatherless midnight as they help vision-impaired individuals see that, while their earthly father may be inept, God is a great father. With God's help, we can help those hurting to see and know that God is a father who will never hurt them, leave them or forget them.

Through our counseling, preaching, modeling, conversations, prayers and programs, we can work with God to remove the blinders. We can help those affected by fatherlessness to see God as

A loving father
A merciful father
A forgiving father
A nurturing father
A healing father
A providing father
An understanding father
A validating father
A protecting father
A patient father
A disciplining father
A knowing father
A trustworthy father
A righteous father
And, most of all, as a *present* father

With people like Jamie, Ticole and John, we can help shed the scales caused by human failure. As Jesus did with the blind man, we can wash the mud off their eyes so they can see the greatness of God their Father.

No one should have to live life without the benefit of a natural and spiritual father. The good news rings loud and clear: There is a good father who wants and loves us all. That father is God.

THE HEALING PATH

Intervention, a program on the A&E network, aired a show involving Rocky Lockridge and his two sons and brother. In 1984, Rocky became the junior lightweight boxing champion of the world after knocking out Roger Mayweather just 98 seconds into the first round. He stood in the middle of the ring on top of the world. With the coveted championship belt fastened around his waist, his arms raised in jubilation and his face beaming with the radiance of a dream come true, there was no stopping him. Now he had it all, according to the world's perspective—all the wine, women and song. And let's not forget the money: millions of dollars lined his accounts. He also married his high school sweetheart, who gave birth to twin boys.

Though his rise to the top was arduous, Rocky's descent was swift. The use of drugs and the pressure of staying on top began to take a toll on him. One night he lost a fight—and the championship belt. As he stepped out of the ring, it was as if he were stepping out of life. His wife packed up the two boys and left him, moving to another city. According to the interview, she was straight as an arrow and had no tolerance for the lifestyle Rocky was living.

Months later Rocky moved to join the family, but the situation was violent and tumultuous. One night, he and his wife were in a domestic squabble, and the police came and hauled Rocky off to jail. That was the last time his boys saw him; when Rocky left the house, he left their lives. He moved to New Jersey and became a crack addict. He was homeless and living miles away from his sons, geographically, emotionally and spiritually.

After fifteen years, his oldest son, Rickey Jr., went to look for his dad and get him help. He coaxed him into coming to a meeting with Rocky's brother and his other son, Lamar. Rocky was unaware that he was about to encounter an intervention. Now we get to the point of the story.

The intervention was one of the most intense and heartbreaking interactions I've ever witnessed. Gut-wrenching were the words that poured out of his sons' hearts. Words marinated in years of abandonment and pain were spoken agonizingly as if they were bemoaned in childbirth. Hear—feel—the words of his pain-filled sons:

From *Intervention* on A&E

Ricky Jr: (weeping) I never lost hope in you. I cried every single day hoping I would see you again. I made it my duty to find you. You have sons who love you and have hope for you and want you in our lives; you owe it to us! I cried myself to sleep every night, longing to see you again.

Lamar: I've waited over fifteen years for this moment. Do you understand this?! I don't know who you are; people tell me you are the champ. The champ of what? Your drug addiction has caused you to see only Rocky the champ. I believe you have forgotten who Rickey Lockridge is? Rickey Lockridge is a father; he is a brother. He's a friend. You replaced all those things with drugs.

You left me and my siblings without a father. You left me looking over my shoulder at every Black man that walks past me, hoping that it was you. You caused me to hate you with a passion so deep that it flows through my veins like the blood that flows through yours. And still I am here because I know that somewhere deep down in my heart, I still love you. I have no faith in you. Please change my faith in my father.[1]

Rickey Jr. and Lamar have something in common with millions of other people: the undesirable pain inflicted by the sword of an absent or inadequate father. It's what Francis Anfuso calls a father wound. In his book *Father Wounds, Recovering Your Childhood*, Anfuso defines a father wound: "The truth is you and I are wired for perfect love. God is the father we always wanted; the perfect Dad each of us desires and needs. Anything modeled by our earthly parents that misses the mark of God's perfect selfless love can create a father wound."[2] In the blink of an eye, abuse, neglect and abandonment miss the mark of God's selfless love, and there are many Rickys and Lamars to prove it.

We can help those in our churches, ministries and organizations ease the pain of their father wound. I admit that many injuries go much deeper than the scope of this chapter and may require additional professional help. However, from my pastoral experience, I believe that as we pray, counsel, encourage and support father victims to progress in these areas, their pain can be eased and the father wound can be healed.

Admit the Pain

Denial and neglect do not foster healing. Just like everything else, admitting that an issue exists is the first step on the journey toward wholeness. One of the stories I love to preach on is the story of the woman with the issue of blood. For twelve long years, this woman's health, finances and social standing digressed. Her only hope for restoration and healing rests in what she has heard about Jesus Christ. She reasons in her heart that if she could just touch the hem Jesus' garment, her fortunes will change.

Outside her home, she hears the commotion of a bustling crowd. She struggles to make sense of the myriad swirling sounds, voices, footsteps—amid the noise of the pain afflicting her body. Straining to understand, she suddenly comprehends: Jesus is passing by!

In her weakness and with a few dwindling ounces of hope left within her, she presses her way through the crowd and touches Jesus. When her hand touches the Master's dusty garment, something beautiful happens. The source of her suffering ceases to exist.

One aspect that we often fail to communicate about this story is the fact that Jesus asked who touched him and the response that followed.

> "You see the people crowding against you," his disciples answered, "and yet you can ask, Who touched me?" But Jesus kept looking around to see who had done it. Then the woman, knowing what had happened to her, came and fell at his feet and, trembling with fear, told him the whole truth. He said to her, "Daughter, your faith has healed you. Go in peace and be freed from your suffering." (Mk 5:31-34)

Jesus could have allowed this woman to be healed and go on her merry way, but he chose not to. He brought her to a place where she had to acknowledge before him and others the issue that had plagued her for so long. There are many other things I could say about this text, but the point at hand is that Jesus pronounced a blessing of wholeness and healing only after she admitted her source of pain—her issue.

Sometime you hear statements like "I only want to focus on the good parts and not the bad." Or "I don't remember all the stuff that happened; I'm all right now anyway." Yes, there may have been some good times, but the bad times were harsh, and you were wounded as a result. There's nothing wrong with admitting, "I hurt."

As pastors and leaders, we can help fatherless individuals recognize the pain and let them know it's acceptable for them to admit the hurt. We can help them to understand that some of the issues about trust, authority, esteem and commitment stem from the fatherless wound. We can encourage them that admitting the pain is present is a first step on the journey to wholeness.

Forgive

Tina and I nervously and soberly entered the Justice Center. As we approached the unwelcoming fortress-like information booth, the officer said, "Can I help you?"

"Yes," she answered, "my name is Tina Williams, and this is my pastor."

Moments later, a lawyer came and greeted us, and we made our way through all the security checks, metal detectors and interrogation sessions. Then the door opened, and an officer ushered us down a vacant, sterile hallway and seated us in an unusual, cubical room. It was a high-security room with large panels of glass on each wall. The glass walls allowed the guards on the outside to observe the happenings in the room as effectively as the guards inside.

We had come to the Justice Center not for any criminal activity on our part. It was for Tina to have a conversation with the young man who had shot and killed her beloved son.

I remember the night I received the call to come to the hospital. Driving there, I was unaware of the gravity of the situation, but in a matter of moments, I was about to find out. Standing in the hospital were a group of loved ones stricken with shock, disbelief, anger and sadness. When I made eye contact with Tina, there was nothing I could say; all I could do was give her an embrace. I could say or do nothing to fix the desperate situation.

The doctor came into the room where she and I were seated and explained the nature of the wound and that her son was on life support until she had a chance to see him. The doctor tried to prepare us for what we would see in a few moments. She explained to us that they had tried to clean up the wound as best as they could, but we should expect to see some gore.

Then she asked, "Would you like to go back now?"

Tina responded, "Yes, and my pastor will go with me." Honestly, she thought I was holding her up, but in reality, she was holding me up.

We enter the room, and there he was, her beloved son in body only, because his soul had departed.

Moments after Tina and I were seated in the glass security room, a young man in jail garb was escorted in. As he sat, we exchanged greetings, which were as awkward and tense as a novice trying to work with a power line. Then I began to witness a miracle and hear one of the most powerful sermons I've ever heard.

Tina started to talk. "I loved my son, more than you could ever know. Why would you take a gun and extinguish his life? I want to tell you, you have made a mistake, but change your life. I love you and forgive you. Please, young man, turn your life over to Christ, and he will help you become the man, the person, he desires you to be. He will forgive too." And she prayed.

Was Tina in pain? Yes! Was she mourning her son? Yes! Was God giving her strength and grace to forgive the man who had violently altered her life, her kids and their family? Yes! The forgiveness she extended to the young man was genuine.

Those suffering from father wounds have to forgive their fathers to find the freedom and healing they so desperately crave. In the A&E intervention, Lamar told his father, "I hate you with a passion so deep that it flows through my veins, like the blood flows through yours." No one can live a healthy life with the blood of hatred and unforgiveness flowing through their veins.

Some people have to forgive without ever seeing or talking to their father. I read in one case where a woman went to the gravesite of her abusive father and spoke the grief of her heart concerning him over the headstone. She finished by saying, "I forgive you."

It's important for people forgiving their father to understand that they may never receive the response they are expecting or desiring. Some fathers may not ever apologize to their children. Their behavior and neglectful or abusive ways may never change. And in some instances, a maladjusted father may try to place the blame, fault and responsibility on the child. However, despite the father's response, whether positive or negative, giving forgiveness is essential for a person suffering from a father wound to experience health.

Abiding in an unforgiving state keeps a person locked in a prison of pain. Forgiving an absent father opens the door for him or her to walk out of the prison. The failure to forgive keeps people encaged in a cell.

Jesus explains this:

> Then Peter came to Jesus and asked, "Lord, how many times shall I forgive my brother when he sins against me? Up to seven times?"
>
> Jesus answered, "I tell you, not seven times, but seventy-seven times. Therefore, the kingdom of heaven is like a king who wanted to settle accounts with his servants. As he began the settlement, a man who owed him ten thousand talents was brought to him. Since he was not able to pay, the master ordered that he and his wife and his children and all that he had be sold to repay the debt.
>
> "The servant fell on his knees before him. 'Be patient with me,' he begged, 'and I will pay back everything.' The servant's master took pity on him, canceled the debt and let him go.
>
> "But when that servant went out, he found one of his fellow servants who owed him a hundred denarii. He grabbed him and began to choke him. 'Pay back what you owe me!' he demanded.

"His fellow servant fell to his knees and begged him, 'Be patient with me, and I will pay you back.' But he refused. Instead, he went off and had the man thrown into prison until he could pay the debt. When the other servants saw what had happened, they were greatly distressed and went and told their master everything that had happened.

"Then the master called the servant in. 'You wicked servant,' he said, 'I canceled all that debt of yours because you begged me to. Shouldn't you have had mercy on your fellow servant just as I had on you?' In anger his master turned him over to the jailers to be tortured, until he should pay back all he owed.

"This is how my heavenly Father will treat each of you unless you forgive your brother from your heart." (Mt 18:21-35)

I can hear someone saying, "But, Pastor Mark, I didn't do anything; he hurt me!" I understand, and that is the truth. However, wounded people can't allow their fathers to hurt them over and over. They must forgive to come out of the prison of unforgiveness.

How to Forgive

Forgiving can be a challenging and difficult act. Sometimes it comes easily, but at other times, it's a life-or-death struggle. To help a person who has been wounded by his or her father, read the following not as something to aid just him or her. Also look at it in light of unforgiveness you may have toward your own father or in light of your own experience of forgiving someone who hurt you deeply.

- *Forgiving a person who has injured you is not optional.* This is worth reiterating. If you are going to heal, the tumor of unforgiveness has to be cut out of your life. This may be a harsh reality, but by God's grace you have to come to terms with that biblical truth. Remember, it's the truth that sets you free. And the truth is we are to forgive.

- *Forgiving is not based on emotions.* Forgiveness is an act of the will. You choose to forgive a person. But the emotions may not follow immediately, just as a flesh wound doesn't heal overnight. When you bandage and disinfected a wound, it's still tender, but the decision to do something facilitates the healing. When you make the decision, say with your mouth and in your heart, "I forgive my father," healing will begin. Don't sweat the feelings; make the decision. The emotions will come at some point.

- *Forgiving doesn't demand that you place yourself back in an abusive situation.* Some will counsel that if you forgive, just forget, and subject yourself to the harm all over again. Forgiveness says, I forgive you for the act you committed against me. Wisdom says, I'm not going to be stupid enough to put myself in that predicament again.

- *Forgiveness requires that you forgive yourself.* In some cases, I've talked to fatherless victims who believe they are to blame. They think that if they had been a better child or done something different, Dad would still be there. Not the case! You are not to blame. Therefore, forgive yourself of any false sense of guilt or condemnation. You are the victim, not the perpetrator.

- *Forgiveness requires wisdom.* Wisdom shows you the best way to give forgiveness. One method doesn't fit all circumstances. For example, if you have a violently abusive father, the best method may not be to have a face-to-face interaction with him by yourself. Maybe you need to take someone with you or send a letter or make a phone call. In some cases, forgiveness is given in the privacy of your heart, between you and God alone. God will give wisdom through prayer and counsel as to what your action plan should be.

- *Forgiving requires God's help.* As in the case of Mrs. Williams, there was no way on earth the love and forgiveness she gave to her son's killer could have been given in her own strength. God helped her, and God will help you. He will help you through your prayers, through the wise counsel of others and by his Spirit that lives in your heart. Yes, it may be difficult to forgive, but you don't have to do it by yourself. Your heavenly Father, who commands you to forgive, will give you all the grace and help you need to be forgiving.

The time has come for the fatherless to exit their cells. The key is in their hand, and with your and God's help, they can use it and forgive. They can shed the captivity of their prison warden, and enjoy the liberty their heavenly Father has to offer them.

Receiving Acceptance/Validation

A group of thirty to forty men of all ages sat in a room in the presence of God and one another, sharing joys and deep aches of the soul. Sitting in the chair, with his face buried in his hand, his head occasionally rising to gasp a breath—Jason sobbed, "Why don't he want me? I don't understand why my dad don't want me. Why don't he want me, man?" None of the men or young men in the room had the answer to his question. But most of us knew the problem: young Jason was crying out for the acceptance of his father.

As I stated in chapter five, "Equipping Men to Be Fathers," kids need to know they are wanted and valued by their dad (the redemption rite). A father's stamp of approval is an essential validation a child needs. Without the stamp, Jason's cry may ring from his heart throughout his life.

Finding acceptance is the same as forgiveness. Some fathers do not ever validate their children, giving them the acceptance they crave. Sometimes a father wakes up and does the right thing, but if he doesn't, we can still help the fatherless find the acceptance they need.

A powerful passage that speaks to the issue of acceptance and gives insight into where a person in need may find validation is Matthew 3:16-17: "As soon as Jesus was baptized, he went up out of the water. At that moment heaven was opened, and he saw the Spirit of God descending like a dove and lighting on him. And a voice from heaven said, 'This is my Son, whom I love; with him I am well pleased.'"

This verse speaks volumes on the importance of a father validating and accepting his son. In this public event, God the Father makes two significant gestures on behalf of his Son. First, he touches him. John said he saw the Spirit descending like a dove and resting on Jesus. The Spirit in this instance was not manifested in fire or a strong wind, but in the gentleness and tenderness of a life-giving dove. What John saw and articulated was the visible act of God the Father tenderly touching and validating his Son. Acceptance requires a father's touch.

Second, God the Father spoke words. His words addressed three needs that foster acceptance:

1. *Relationship.* God says, "This my son! He belongs to me and I belong to Him. I take ownership."

2. *Affection.* God says, "He's my son whom I love. He has my heart and loyalty. I will be faithful to him."

3. *Delight.* God says, "In him I am well pleased." At this point in Jesus' life, he hasn't preached, taught, worked any miracles, gone to the cross or risen from the grave. Therefore, the Father is not pleased with his Son by virtue of what he had done, but by virtue of who he is.

Those seeking acceptance need to understand that God their heavenly Father validates them. They need to experience his gentle touch and hear him loudly speak the words in their heart for the universe to hear, "You are my child. I love you. You are my delight."

A person can experience this acceptance and validation through a vital and authentic relationship with the Lord Jesus Christ. Jesus' prayer was for the Father to make us one as he and the Father are one (Jn 17). If we are one with Christ, we are one with the Father. That unity affords us the unique blessing of the validation that fosters the acceptance that only the heavenly Father can give. Ephesians 1:3-6 encourages all of us in our quest for acceptance:

> Blessed be the God and Father of our Lord Jesus Christ, who has blessed us with every spiritual blessing in the heavenly places in Christ, just as He chose us in Him before the foundation of the world, that we should be holy and without blame before Him in love, having predestined us to *adoption as sons* by Jesus Christ to Himself, according to the good pleasure of His will, to the praise of the glory of His grace, by which He made us *accepted* in the Beloved. (NKJV, emphasis added)

In Christ, we have all the validation and acceptance that is heavenly possible. As pastors and leaders, we encourage people in so many areas to trust God and rely on his Word. You can do the same for the fatherless who are in need of acceptance. You can help them embrace the truth and reality that, while their mother and father may forsake them, God will never leave them. We need to preach this as loud as the cry of their hearts: You are accepted in the Beloved!

One more note on acceptance. After Jason finished his lament, one of the older men in the group walked over and hugged him. As loud as Jason was crying, he exclaimed, "I want you, and I will be your dad. You are my son!" In that moment, Jason received a word and a touch from a surrogate father who brought a measure of healing in his life. Chapter six, "Mentoring the Fatherless," explains how we can facilitate this. On another positive note, Jason's biological father has been making some steps, too, and their relationship is improving.

Finding a Place of Support

George Merriweather, the pastor of Northeast Community Fellowship Foursquare Church in Portland, started a small group for men who were grappling with father pain. George himself lost his father at an early age. So he was not just the facilitator of the group, he was a participant as well. For about eight months, twenty or so men gathered to share their stories, pray for one another and study Francis Anfuso's *Father Wounds*.

In their time together, the men realized they were not alone in their pain. Having a man sitting directly across from them or next to them and understanding their suffering was a great comfort and encouragement to the men of the group. One participant, Montreal, said that he was helped by the discussion they had about what was missing in their lives due to their father's absence. The practical skills, such as how to treat their wives and children, were also very helpful. He felt he found healing and became a better dad as a result.

The support of others is important. God's miracles are not all instantaneous; many find fruition in the context of a loving and supportive community of others. Out of the tomb Lazarus came, but he needed to ask people to take off his grave clothes (Jn 11:38-44). Sometimes fatherless men and women need others to help unravel them. Encouraging or providing avenues in your church or ministry can aid in helping the hurting.

Embracing God

The psalmist writes, "My father and mother walked out and left me, but God took me in" (Ps 27:10 Message). All those who are hurting due to the walking out of a father, or even a mother, need to know this: God will take them in. They may ask, "Take me in where?" Our answer is, "Our heavenly Father will take you into the embrace of his heart and arms forever. He will never hurt or orphan you. Call out to him, and he will hear you. Cry out to him, and he will answer you. Long for him, and he will satisfy you. Pour your pain out, and he will hear you."

Scripture describes why and how acutely God is aware of pain and what he desires to do about it.

> The LORD said, "I have indeed seen the misery of my people in Egypt. I have heard them crying out because of their slave drivers, and I am concerned about their suffering. So I have come down to rescue them from the hand of the Egyptians and to bring them up out of that land into a good and spacious land, a land flowing with milk and honey—the home of the Canaanites, Hittites, Amorites, Perizzites, Hivites and Jebusites." (Ex 3:7-8)

These verses tell us that God is a seeing God who knows our misery. He is a hearing God who hears our cry. God is a concerned God who comes down to help us in our suffering to bring us into a good, new, spacious place. God knows all about us, and he is reaching out to embrace us. We can relax, trust and fall into the embrace of our heavenly Father. And we can help others do the same.

Bernis Dorsey's Story

Brother Dorsey, as he is so affectionately called at our church and around the city, embraced God in the midst of confusing father pain. Here's his story:

Bernis woke up and looked around the room. It was stifling hot on that summer morning. He pushed his brothers away from him in the bed to get some breathing room. "What am I doing here?" he asked himself. "Why do we have to live like this?"

Bernis lived in a house with only two rooms. There were nine of them living there: his two brothers and four sisters, mother and grandmother. There was no electricity, no running water, no telephone. What Bernis *did* have plenty of was anger and hurt. He might have been only twelve years old, but he knew that what his dad had done was wrong.

His dad had left the family when Bernis was only one. And he had never sent his mother any money to support his family, had never sent him any presents for his birthday or Christmas, and had never come to visit him.

His mother had told him something very exciting the day before. "You'll be going to take a drive tomorrow and go to meet your dad." Really? He would finally be able to ask his dad the questions that had been on his mind for many years.

When Bernis reached his father's house, he waited for the chance to be alone with him. When that time came, he looked at his dad and asked, "Why did you never come see me? And why did you never send Mom any money to take care of us?" He anxiously awaited the response that would finally answer his questions.

But his dad said nothing. There was only silence. He didn't answer Bernis that day, and he never did answer him in the years to follow. What Bernis did hear, however, was the woman down the street, who said, "Your dad told me your mother was dead."

As it had been before that first visit with his dad, it was as he grew older. The hurt, the pain and the anger continued. It seemed to him that every one of his friends had a father or a stepfather. One of the hardest things for Bernis was when his friends would talk about things they had done with their dads or about gifts that their dads had bought them. Sometimes they would ask him, "How come you don't have a dad? Where is he?"

Bernis saved his tears for the walk home, when no one could see him. As he walked, he wondered, "How come I don't have a dad to play baseball with? How come I don't have a bicycle? How come my mother has to work, take care of Grandmother and raise seven kids all alone?" It made him so angry and sad.

That anger and his desire for things that his friends had led to some wrong actions when he was a teenager. One of those actions involved a horn that he really wanted, so that he could make music in the school band. Bernis was determined he was going to get that horn no matter what. So he devised a plan. He stole a check from the man he was working for and forged it to buy the horn. Fortunately, though the forgery was caught, things worked out so that he didn't end up in a juvenile correction center.

To see Bernis as he is today is to witness God's amazing healing power. Happily married for over forty years, he has four children and six grandchildren. He serves as a pastor at our church, where he is widely respected and greatly loved. It's a rare Sunday when you don't see him praying for one or more young men after the service. And if you look around the church, it would be hard to identify a family that has not been blessed by his prayers, witness or wisdom.

How did the lonely, angry teenager come to be the person he is today? Bernis identifies a couple of key turning points. One was when he accepted the Lord Jesus Christ as his savior in his early twenties. Though he had attended church as a child and heard the Word, his salvation brought new strength and peace as he matured.

Not too long after his salvation, Bernis enlisted in the military. He says he met men of integrity in the military, men who reached out to him as teachers and mentors. Prior to the military, there had been no man to teach him how to be a responsible man. Bernis also credits his mother as having an important role in his ability to move forward. She taught him over time how important it is to "love your dad as best you can" and "remember, you don't have to be a man like your dad."

After the military, Bernis had jobs with both GE and DuPont. During his years with DuPont, he began his work as a vocational pastor. He eventually moved into full-time pastoring and has served in three churches over the past thirty-two years (as the primary pastor in two of those churches). During those years, he has had a positive impact on hundreds who were fatherless.

Bernis ministers to the fatherless in many ways. He serves as a spiritual dad, so that those hurting can experience the comfort and teaching of an earthly father. He counsels many one-to-one, walking them through tough challenges. He teaches them through his sermons and classes, and he provides a clear understanding of God as their Father. He shares his own testimony, helping them to be encouraged. And he earnestly prays for them.

Being aware of Bernis's childhood and where he is now helps us to see how important it is to encourage, teach, love and pray for the fatherless. We never know what God has in store for them as they heal, grow and find their purpose in life. Recently Bernis and his wife travelled back east, where his family had planned for a special celebration of his life. As he heard his family testify to how he had been a father to them, he recalled something the Lord had told him many years earlier: "Even though you didn't have a father to father you, I have shown you that I am your father. And I have made you a father to many."

Many people today are in Bernis's shoes. Their father has left, and their living conditions are subpar. They live daily under the haunting shadow posed by the question "Why don't you love or care for me?" They battle with anger and frustration, feeling as if a volcano is erupting within. The pain they bear seems unyielding and inescapable. But there is good news. God healed Bernis's heart, and he can heal the hearts of those you know who have been hurt by fatherly neglect and abuse.

It's time to wipe away some of the tears and time to cut the ribbon on the vessel so those hurt by earthly fathers can embark on a new journey. We as the church community are there to help, but most of all, God is here to help us, and he will.

My Prayer for the Fatherless

Father, today I ask that you would pull back the layers of pain caused by the careless hands of earthly fathers. Pour oil into the wounded and broken places in the hearts of little boys and little girls—both young and old. Fill their being with the warmth of your love. Obliterate the darkness and scattered dreams of days, months and years of unfulfilled expectations. Allow them to find a home in your fatherly embrace. When they feel alone, let them know and experience your presence. Father, speak loudly into their hearts: You are my child and I love you. Assure them of your plan for their lives, your plan to give them a hope and future. Let them know that they have a good Father—You. Amen!

10

HOW DO I GET STARTED?

My friend's little girl sat sobbing in the middle of her floor. His wife had told her to clean her room, but she had made such a mess, she was overwhelmed and didn't know where to start. Her mother went into the room and showed the troubled little six-year-old how to start cleaning up her room by picking up one thing at a time. After half an hour or so, and with a little help from Mom, the room was clean. Thank God for good moms!

With the fatherless issue, it would be easy to look around our churches, community and neighborhoods and just sob at the enormity of the problem. Like the little girl, we are prone to say, "There is no way I can make a difference. Where do I even start?"

Allow me to alter an old adage: "Ministry to the fatherless is not a sprint, but a marathon." The following admonitions are a few snippets of pastoral advice to aid you on your journey of ministering to the fatherless. I hope these encourage you not for the short race, but for the long haul.

Begin. The fatherless problem is enormous. You may face gnawing anxiety that comes from feeling you need to minister to the fatherless in a complex or big way. If you have the resources to conduct such a venture and God leads you in that direction, go for it. However, don't feel that the call is either to do something big or to do nothing at all. Start where you can. Remember, David slew Goliath with a sling and a stone, and Jesus fed the five thousand with two fish and five loaves of bread. Identify one thing you can do, and do it. Understand that your small step is a giant step in the life of a fatherless individual. Your tool is in your hand—start working.

> Do not despise these small beginnings, for the LORD rejoices
> to see the work begin, to see the plumb line in Zerubbabel's
> hand. (Zech 4:10 NLT)

Be encouraged. I don't want to give any false illusions. While ministering to those affected by fatherlessness can be rewarding, the process can be arduous and messy. There will be seasons when you feel as if you're banging your head against a brick wall. Your efforts and prayers at times will seem ineffective and unsuccessful. You will find yourself working with an individual who takes three steps forward and nine steps back. You might ask yourself, "Is it worth it? Is what I am doing even necessary?" Emphatically, yes! Those times are to be expected and are a part of the process. You will have to encourage yourself during those valleys so you won't give up and throw in the towel. The fact that you're experiencing rough terrain is a positive indication that you're making progress. Encourage yourself and keep going.

> Have I not commanded you? Be strong and courageous. Do
> not be terrified; do not be discouraged, for the LORD your
> God will be with you wherever you go. (Josh 1:9)
>
> Let us not become weary in doing good, for at the proper
> time we will reap a harvest if we do not give up. (Gal 6:9)

Be connected. When Jesus sent out the disciples, he sent them out in twos. Why? Because there's strength in partnerships. As you work with the fatherless, find someone who will stand with you. This person may not necessarily do what you do, but he or she is there to pray with you and give you moral support and encouragement. With modern modes of communications, your support partner could live next door or in Timbuktu.

The benefit of having a like-minded person on your team is invaluable. Don't try to minister alone. Ask God to give you a support partner, and he will. With a support partner, you'll last longer and go further.

> Two are better than one, because they have a good return for their work: If one falls down, his friend can help him up. But pity the man who falls and has no one to help him up! Also, if two lie down together, they will keep warm. But how can one keep warm alone? Though one may be overpowered, two can defend themselves. A cord of three strands is not quickly broken. (Eccles 4:9-12)

Be equipped. Continue to learn all you can about fatherlessness and ways to minister to those affected. Talk with and learn from others who are ministering in this area. Read books and listen to CDs on how to minister to the various needs fatherless individuals have. Study the Scriptures, and ask God to give you wisdom and insight. Do all you can to grow and develop; the more you equip yourself, the more ways God can use you to father the fatherless.

> Study to shew thyself approved unto God, a workman that needeth not to be ashamed, rightly dividing the word of truth. (2 Tim 2:15 KJV)

Be thankful. Serving the fatherless is not an obligation, but a gift and opportunity from the Lord. Therefore, the posture of your heart should be that of thanksgiving. Allow your heart to overflow with gratitude to the Lord for allowing you to participate in a life-changing ministry to the fatherless. Be deliberate about keeping a song in your heart and praise on your lips to God.

He has blessed you with the wonderful privilege of collaborating with him to bless the lives of the fatherless. A thankful heart is a loving heart, and a loving heart represents God's heart.

> I thank Christ Jesus our Lord, who has given me strength, that he considered me faithful, appointing me to his service. Even though I was once a blasphemer and a persecutor and a violent man, I was shown mercy because I acted in ignorance and unbelief. The grace of our Lord was poured out on me abundantly, along with the faith and love that are in Christ Jesus. (1 Tim 1:12-14)

Be joyful. Fatherlessness is a serious issue, but serving the fatherless is a joyous experience. The relationships you build with others and the beauty of seeing lives transformed are the substance joyful smiles are made of. Serving with joy allows you not to take yourself too seriously. It also allows you not to place an unrealistic onus on yourself, as if you are the sole answer for the entire fatherless dilemma.

When I was in seminary, one of my professors made a comment about some of the guys he went to school with: "The guys who played Ping-Pong and enjoyed life during their seminary days are still in the ministry today. The guys who were so serious and never came up for air or to have some fun are not in the ministry today." The point is well taken: we are to have a measure of joy serving the Lord. Enjoy serving the fatherless. Be joyful and have some fun whenever you can.

> Nehemiah said, "Go and enjoy choice food and sweet drinks, and send some to those who have nothing prepared. This day is sacred to our Lord. Do not grieve, for the joy of the Lord is your strength." (Neh 8:10)

Be smart. Being smart means that you don't bite off more than you can chew and that you rest when you need to. My wife constantly preaches to me the Need for Rest sermon. The reason I need to hear that message constantly is because there is always so much to do. As I stated earlier, the magnitude of the fatherless issue requires more than one person, church or ministry to fix. It also commands more hours in the day, week or month than you have to give. The work will always be there, so pace yourself.

In the words of Kenny Rogers, know when to hold up, know when to fold up, know when to walk away and know when to run. In my vernacular, know when to rest. Take the time to regroup and unplug when you need to. It's okay! After all, God rested, and if he needed to rest, I believe we do as well.

> The LORD replied, "My Presence will go with you, and I will give you rest." (Ex 33:14)

Be tenacious. Simply put—don't quit! Keep on going until you reach the finish line. Starting is good, but finishing is better. Possess the internal conviction and determination that you are to keep at it until God says differently. God will help you begin, and he is faithful to help you finish.

> Not that I have already obtained all this, or have already been made perfect, but I press on to take hold of that for which Christ Jesus took hold of me. Brothers, I do not consider myself yet to have taken hold of it. But one thing I do: Forgetting what is behind and straining toward what is ahead, I press on toward the goal to win the prize for which God has called me heavenward in Christ Jesus. (Phil 3:12-14)

Be prayerful. Working with the fatherless requires more than your own natural ability. Staying in communion with God bridges the gap between your lack and inability and God's surplus and ability. Pray for and about everything. Pray for yourself, those you are working with and whatever else burdens your heart or mind. Prayer is your lifeline for ministry to the fatherless.

Do not be anxious about anything, but in everything, by prayer and petition, with thanksgiving, present your requests to God. And the peace of God, which transcends all understanding, will guard your hearts and your minds in Christ Jesus. (Phil 4:6-7)

Believe. Working with the fatherless requires faith. And faith provides the substructure for the work you will do with the fatherless. It's necessary and essential. Faith is required to believe that God will use you to make a difference in the lives of the fatherless. Faith is necessary if you are to believe it's possible for troubled lives to experience transformation. Faith is crucial to enable you to keep going despite the obstacles and discouragements you encounter. Faith is central to believing that God is with you and that he will give you everything you need to do the job he has called you to do. Faith is believing God will perform all he has promised. As the old hymn eloquently states, only believe!

Then Jesus said, "Did I not tell you that if you believed, you would see the glory of God?" (Jn 11:40)

Go ahead and get started. And go the distance!

Epilogue

A NEW STORY

If you were to come to Life Change Christian Center on any given day, one of the young men you would find hustling and bustling around the church is Shawn. You could find him helping out in the office or at one of the daily prayer meetings. Without a doubt, you could find him working with the youth of the church and in the community. Shawn's life is a blessing to many, and he's an example to the youth of what it means to live for Christ. God has and is performing a wonderful work of grace in the life and heart of this young man.

And without a doubt the hand of God is on Shawn to do great things. He is the type of young man that you wish the church was full of. The question you ask yourself is, where do young men of this caliber come from? Let me tell you where Shawn came from.

Shawn was born to a single, teenage girl. When he arrived, his biological father was not convinced that this little boy was his. Shawn says that his father sent a relative to the hospital to see if he was his child or not. The report came back positive. Throughout the first nine years of his life, his mom and dad had a couple of brief stints of being together. They even tried marriage on one occasion, but it lasted only a few months due to drugs and gambling.

So Shawn's first nine years were spent without the emotional closeness of a father. When he was nine, he went to live with his grandmother and his father. Though his father was physically present and provided materially, there was no emotional connection or communication.

During his teen years, Shawn was a well-mannered kid, but he loved the party and drinking scene. He was free to come and go as he pleased, with no curfew or restrictions—and we know how dangerous that can be. Although he had the freedom most teens dream of, inside of him a silent, strong and destructive force began to swell. Heavy weekend drinking soon extended through the rest of the week. He says he was always drunk, and his skin started changing colors.

During this time, Shawn kept having a dream. In his dream, something would tell him he would live forever, and then all of a sudden he'd be in a space enveloped with darkness, a place he knew was a place of death.

One Sunday he found himself sitting in a worship service at Life Change Christian Center and felt that the message was speaking directly to him. For several months he came to church regularly but didn't make a decision for Christ. He determined that on Christmas night, he was going to have his last round of partying before he surrendered to Christ. But something told him not to go.

That night, while Shawn sat in a café, a young man came over to his table to pick a fight. The young man slugged Shawn in the face twice and then stepped back, pulled up his shirt and reached for a gun. Fortunately, a security guard walked in at that moment, and the young man with the gun ran from the scene. Immediately Shawn and his family began to make plans to exact revenge. But in the midst of the planning, Shawn began to pray for the young man. When he finished praying that night, he repented of his sins and came to faith in Christ.

I asked Shawn how the church has helped him in light of his father situation. He replied that though he knows his parents love him, church was the first place he experienced unconditional love and acceptance. He has watched and been mentored by godly male role models, and the Word of God has helped him to erase false images of what it means to be a man.

Shawn's relationship with Christ brought the answer to his nightmare. No longer would he live in the darkness, but he would now have eternal life in Christ. Shawn is preparing to be married in a few weeks. He's marrying a wonderful Christian girl, and they both have hearts to minister to hurting and broken young people.

There are a lot of Shawns out there, and you and your church can make a difference. Will you be one of those people who love the fatherless? Will you be one of those churches that ministers to the fatherless? Will you be one of those ministries that heals the fatherless? If so, God will help you. You can make a difference. *We* can make a difference.

Acknowledgments

Many people are owed a great debt of gratitude for their invaluable contribution to this work. To begin with, I would like to thank my wife, Marla. In our journey of life through the highs and the lows, she has always been a great source of comfort, strength, wisdom and encouragement to me. Her companionship makes the sometimes-arduous road of life much easier and pleasant to travel. I love you, Honey!

To the 4 m's, Micah, Michelle, McKenzie and Myles, you guys are awesome, and Daddy loves you a whole bunch!

Thank you Life Change family; it has been a joy to serve as your pastor for the last twenty-four-plus years. Thanks for all the prayers, words of encouragement, and your dedication to God. Thanks for being a community of faith that is making a difference in the world for the sake of Jesus Christ. A special thanks to all our staff and elders, Jerrell Waddell, Bernis Dorsey, Andrew Miller, Cathy Rhodes and all of our great leaders—I sincerely appreciate you all. Thanks to Patsy Lindsey for your help and insight.

Thank you Dr. MaryKate Morse and Dr. Charles Conniry. Your constant help and encouragement has been extremely influential not only in the completion of this book but also in my life and our church as well. Thank you for serving to make George Fox Seminary an institution that has affected my life and ministry.

Thank you InterVarsity Press for giving me an opportunity to put the burden of my heart in print, and for the hope of helping fatherless individuals to find healing and wholeness. Thank you, Cindy Bunch, for making the process enjoyable.

Most of all, thank you God for being a loving Father and for sending your Son Jesus Christ so that every person on the earth can experience the love of Father God.

Appendix A

RESOURCES

Equipping fathers. Below is a list of resources that you can use to equip fathers in your ministry. Also, remember to use the Bible; God has a lot of good information in there too.

Canfield, Ken R. *The Seven Secrets of Effective Fathers: Becoming the Father Your Children Need.* Wheaton, Ill.: Tyndale, 1992.

Cornwall, Judson. *My Father and I: How the Bible Teaches Fatherhood.* Hagerstown, Md.: McDougal Publishing, 1998.

Cothern, Clark. *At the Heart of Every Great Father: The Heart of Jesus.* Sisters, Ore.: Multnomah, 1998.

Parker, Matthew. *African American Churches: Teaching Our Men, Reaching Our Fathers.* Detroit, Mich.: Institute for Black Family Development, 2002.

Strong, Mark E. *The Men's Series.* Portland, Ore.: Life Change Christian Center, 2010. <www.lifechangecc.org>.

The National Center for Fathering, <www.fathers.com>, is an educational organization that provides research-based training and resources to equip men to effectively meet the needs of their children.

The National Fatherhood Initiative, <www.fatherhood.org>, is an organization that provides a wealth of resources and curriculum for equipping fathers.

Mentoring

The Mentoring Project
P.O. Box 12090, Portland, OR 97271
(503) 894-8076 <www.thementoringproject.org>

Gorsuch, Geoff. *Brothers! Calling Men into Vital Relationships.* Colorado Springs: NavPress, 1994.

Kreider, Larry. *The Cry for Spiritual Mothers and Fathers.* Ephrata, Penn.: House to House Publications, 2000.

Maxwell, John. *Mentoring 101: What Every Leader Needs to Know.* Nashville: Thomas Nelson, 2008.

Stoddard, David A., with Robert A. Tamasy. *The Heart of Mentoring: Ten Proven Principles to Develop People to Their Fullest Potential.* Colorado Springs: NavPress, 2003.

Hendricks, Howard. *Building Character in a Mentoring Relationship, As Iron Sharpens Iron.* Chicago: Moody Press, 1995.

The life of Jesus as recorded in the Gospels

The relationship of Paul and Timothy in 1 and 2 Timothy

Appendix B

SCRIPTURES ON FATHERLESSNESS

God's concern for the fatherless and the community of faith's role and responsibility:
Exodus 22:22
Deuteronomy 10:18
Deuteronomy 14:29
Deuteronomy 16:11
Deuteronomy 24:17-21
Deuteronomy 26:12
Deuteronomy 27:19
Job 22:9
Job 29:12
Job 31:17
Psalm 10:14
Psalm 10:18
Psalm 68:5
Psalm 82:3
Psalm 146:9
Proverbs 23:10
Isaiah 1:17, 23
Isaiah 10:2
Jeremiah 7:6
Jeremiah 49:11
Hosea 14:3
Zechariah 7:10
Malachi 3:5
John 14:8
Ephesians 6:4
1 and 2 Timothy
James 1:27

NOTES

Introduction

[1]David Blankenhorn, *Fatherless America: Confronting Our Most Urgent Social Problem* (New York: HarperPerennial, 1995), p. 1.

[2]David Popenoe, *Life Without Father* (New York: Free Press, 1996), p. 3.

[3]The National Fatherhood Initiative, *Father Facts*, 6th ed. (Germantown, Md., 2011), p. 27.

[4]James A. Levine and Edward W. Pitt, *New Expectations: Community Strategies for Responsible Fatherhood* (New York: Families and Work Institute, 1995), p. 27.

Chapter 1: Father, Where Are You?

[1]Kevin Peraino and Evan Thomas, "Father, Where Art Thou?" *Newsweek*, January 27, 2003, pp. 54-56.

[2]David Popenoe, *Life Without Father* (New York: Free Press, 1996), p. 21.

[3]Donna L. Franklin, *Ensuring Inequality* (New York: Oxford University Press, 1997), p. 99.

[4]Ibid.

[5]Popenoe, *Life Without Father*, p. 124.

[6]Ibid., p. 125.

[7]David Blankenhorn, *Fatherless America: Confronting Our Most Urgent Social Problem* (New York: HarperPerennial, 1995), p. 52.

[8]Ibid., p. 53.

[9]Franklin, *Ensuring Inequality*, p. 114.

[10]Ibid., pp. 114-15.

[11]Ibid., p. 115.

[12]Cynthia R. Daniels, ed., *Lost Fathers* (New York: St. Martin's Press, 1998), p. 2.

[13]Blankenhorn, *Fatherless America*, p. 22.

[14]Ibid.

[15]Ibid., pp. 22-23.

[16]Wade F. Horn and Tom Sylvester, *Father Facts*, 4th ed. (Gaithersburg, Md.: The National Fatherhood Initiative, 2002), p. 23.

[17]The National Fatherhood Initiative, *Father Facts*, 6th ed. (Germantown, Md., 2011), p. 18.

[18]Jonetta Rose Barras, *Whatever Happened to Daddy's Little Girl?* (New York: Ballantine, 2000), p. 45.

[19]Elizabeth M. Perse, *Media Effects and Society* (Mahwah, N.J.: Lawrence Erlbaum Associates, 2001), p. 56.

[20]James A. Levine and Edward W. Pitt, *New Expectations: Community Strategies for Responsible Fatherhood* (New York: Families and Work Institute, 1995), p. 13.

[21]Ibid.

[22]"Etheridge and Crosby Talk," *60 Minutes*, February 11, 2009 <www.cbsnews.com/stories/2000/01/17/60II/main150369.shtml>.

[23]Maggie Gallagher, "Father Hunger," in *Lost Fathers*, ed. Cynthia R. Daniels (New York: St. Martin's Press, 1998), p. 178.

[24]Terri L. Orbuch, Arland Thorton and Jennifer Cancio, "Marital Disruptions and Parent Child Relationships: Interventions and Policies on Fatherhood," in *Fatherhood Research Interventions and Policies*, eds. H. Elizabeth Peters, et al. (New York: Hayworth Press, 2000), p. 227.

[25]M. Belinda Tucker and Claudia Mitchell-Kernan, *The Decline in Marriage Among African Americans: Causes, Consequences and Policy Implications* (New York: Russell Sage Foundation, 1995), pp. 16-18.

[26]Ellis Cose, "The Black Gender Gap," *Newsweek*, March 3, 2003, pp. 46-51.

[27]Haki R. Madubuti, *Black Men Obsolete, Single, Dangerous? The Afrikan American Family in Transition* (Chicago: Third World Press, 1991), p. 61.

[28]Janet Dewart, ed., *The State of Black America 1990* (New York: National Urban League, 1990), p. 92.

[29]Cynthia R. Daniels, "Growing up Without a Father," in *Lost Fathers,* ed. Cynthia R. Daniels (New York: St. Martin's Press, 1998), p. 94.

[30]Ibid., p. 170.

[31]Popenoe, *Life Without Father,* p. 27.

[32]Hanso Group LLC, *Very Local Data* <verylocal.com/cities/Or/portland>, accessed March 22, 2012.

[33]Horn and Sylvester, *Father Facts,* p. 31.

[34]Dewart, *State of Black America,* p. 91.

[35]Franklin, *Ensuring Inequality,* p. 165.

[36]David Claerbaut, *Urban Ministry* (Grand Rapids: Zondervan, 1983), p. 151.

[37]Tucker and Michell-Kernan, *Decline in Marriage,* p. 38.

[38]Dorothy Roberts, "The Absent Black Father," in *Lost Fathers,* ed. Cynthia R. Daniels (New York: St. Martin's Press, 1998), p. 148.

[39]Tucker and Mitchell-Kernan, *Decline in Marriage,* p. 38.

[40]Ibid., p. 46. The author changes the dialect so the reader can hear the slave's own words express the pain of broken and separated families.

[41]Lee A. Beaty, "Effects of Paternal Absence on Male Adolescents' Peer Relationship and Self Image," *Adolescence* 30, no. 120 (Winter 1995): 873.

[42]Donald W. Swan, "Influence of Father Absence and Satisfaction with Parents on Selected Measures of Nurturant Fathering" (PsyD diss., George Fox College, 1996), p. 61.

[43]Jennifer Hamer, "What African American Noncustodial Fathers Say Inhibits and Enhances Their Involvement With Children," *Western Journal of Black Studies* 22 (Summer 1998): 120-25.

[44]Horn and Sylvester, *Father Facts,* p. 128.

[45]Ibid., p. 44.

[46]Roberts, "The Absent Black Father," p. 150.

[47]Mathew Parker, *Teaching Our Men, Reaching Our Fathers* (Detroit: Institute for Black Family Development, 2002), p. 55.

CHAPTER 2: THE IMPACT OF FATHERLESSNESS

[1]Leighton Ford, *Transforming Leadership: Jesus' Way of Creating Vision, Shaping Values and Empowering Change* (Downers Grove, Ill.: InterVarsity Press, 1991), p. 41.

[2]Charnetta Hutson and Chanessa Jackson, "Daddy's Girl," 2000, Portland. Used with permission.

[3]Jonetta Rose Barras, *Whatever Happened to Daddy's Little Girl?* (New York: Ballantine, 2000), p. 5.

[4]Donald W. Swan, "Influence of Father Absence and Satisfaction with Parents on Selected Measures of Nurturant Fathering" (PsyD diss., George Fox College, 1996), pp. 53-54.

[5]Robert S. McGee, *Father Hunger* (Ann Arbor, Mich.: Vine Books, 1993), p. 17.

[6]Ibid., pp. 17-18.

[7]Maggie Gallagher, "Father Hunger," in *Lost Fathers*, ed. Cynthia R. Daniels (New York: St. Martin's Press, 1998), p. 165.

[8]Curtis Kimbrough, *How I Got Over!* (Portland, Ore.: AYWN Publications, 2001), pp. 13-17.

[9]Wade F. Horn and Tom Sylvester, *Father Facts*, 4th ed. (Gaithersburg, Md.: The National Fatherhood Initiative, 2002), p. 131.

[10]Ibid., pp. 37-38.

[11]Timothy S. Grall, "Custodial Mothers and Fathers and Their Child Support: 2007" (November 2009), Washington, D.C., US Census Bureau <www.census.gov/prod/2009pubs/p60-237.pdf>.

[12]Kris Kissman, "Noncustodial Fatherhood: Research Trends and Issues," *Journal of Divorce and Remarriage* 1-2 (1997): 78.

[13]Ibid., pp. 140-42.

[14]Franklin B. Krohn and Zoe Bogan, "The Effects Absent Fathers Have on Female Development and College Attendance," *College Student Journal* 35, no. 4 (December 2001), p. 602.

[15]E. Mavis Hetherington, *Coping with Divorce, Single Parenting and*

Remarriage: A Risk and Resiliency Perspective, ed. Sara L. McLanahan (Mahwah, N.J.: Lawrence Erlbaum Associates, 1999), p. 122.

[16]Krohn and Bogan, "Effects Absent Fathers Have," p. 607.

[17]Susan Faludi, "Ghetto Star: 'Monster' Kody Scott and the Culture of Ornament," *LA Weekly*, October 6, 1999, pp. 8-14.

[18]Elaine H. Rodney and Robert Mupier, "Behavioral Differences Between African American Male Adolescents with Biological Fathers and Those Without Biological Fathers in the Home," *Journal of Black Studies* 30 (September 1999) <www.ephost@epnet.com>, accessed October 17, 2002.

[19]Ibid.

[20]Deborah A. Salem, Marc A. Zimmerman and Paul C. Notaro, "The Effects of Family Structure, Family Process and Father Involvement on Psychosocial Outcomes Among African American Adolescents," *Family Relations* 47 (October 1998) <www.ephost@epnet.com>, accessed October 17, 2002.

[21]David Popenoe, *Life Without Father* (New York: Free Press, 1996), pp. 62-63.

[22]Larry Elder, "All My Friends Are Dying," *Human Events* 57 (June 2001): 21.

[23]The National Fatherhood Initiative, *Father Facts*, 6th ed. (Germantown, Md.: 2011), pp. 16, 27.

[24]Lee A. Beaty, "The Effects of Paternal Absence on Male Adolescents' Peer Relationships and Self-Image," *Adolescence* 30 (Winter 1995): 120 <www.ephost@epnet.com>, accessed October 17, 2002.

[25]Sara L. McLanahan, "Growing up Without a Father," in *Lost Fathers*, ed. Cynthia R. Daniels (New York: St. Martin's Press, 1998), pp. 86-87.

[26]Rodney and Mupier, "Behavioral Differences," p. 46.

[27]Sara McLanahan, "Life Without Father: What Happens to the Children?" (working paper, Princeton University, August 15, 2001).

[28]Krohn and Bogan, "Effects Absent Fathers Have," p. 7.

[29]Salem, Zimmerman and Notaro, "The Effects of Family Structure," pp. 16-17.

[30]McLanahan, "Life Without Father," p. 4.

CHAPTER 3: EMBEDDING A CORPORATE FATHERLESS VALUE

[1]David R. Wenzel, "The Fatherhood of God" (MTh thesis, Western Baptist Seminary, 1990), p. 42.

[2]Richard S. Taylor, ed., *Beacon Dictionary of Theology* (Kansas City: Beacon Hill Press, 1983), p. 297.

CHAPTER 5: EQUIPPING MEN TO BE FATHERS

[1]John W. Miller, *Biblical Faith and Fathering: Why We Call God "Father"* (New York: Paulist Press, 1989), p. 72.

[2]Ibid., p. 73.

[3]Ibid., p. 79.

[4]Ibid., p. 78-79.

[5]Ibid., p. 84.

[6]The National Fatherhood Initiative, *Father Facts*, 6th ed. (Germantown, Md., 2011), p. 40.

CHAPTER 6: MENTORING THE FATHERLESS

[1]Paul Stanley, Leighton Ford and Tom Hawkes, *Mentor Training Seminar* (Charlotte, N.C.: Leighton Ford Ministries, 1996), p. 3.

CHAPTER 7: PRAYING FOR THE CHILDREN

[1]E. M. Bounds, *The Reality of Prayer* (Grand Rapids: Baker, 1988), p. 43.

CHAPTER 8: GOD OUR FATHER

[1]Joachim Jeremias, *The Prayers of Jesus* (Philadelphia: Fortress, 1984), p. 29.

[2]Robert Hamerton-Kelly, *God the Father: Theology and Patriarchy in the Teaching of Jesus* (Philadelphia: Fortress, 1979), p. 54.

[3]Colin Brown, ed., *The New International Dictionary of New Testament Theology*, vol. 1 (Grand Rapids: Regency, 1986), p. 615.

[4]D. A. Carson, "Matthew," *The Expositor's Bible Commentary*, vol. 8, ed. Frank E. Gaebelein (Grand Rapids: Regency, 1981), p. 166.

[5]Marianne M. Thompson, *The Promise of the Father: Jesus and God in the New Testament* (Louisville, Ky.: Westminster/John Knox Press, 2000), p. 125.

[6]Hamerton-Kelly, *God the Father*, pp. 89-90.

[7]Ibid., p. 80.

CHAPTER 9: THE HEALING PATH

[1]*Intervention* on A&E <www.aetv.com/intervention/episode-guide/season-7/rocky-113#113>.

[2]Francis Anfuso, *Father Wounds, Recovering Your Childhood* (Roseville, Calif.: Rock of Roseville, 2008), p. 16.

PRAXIS

EQUIPPING LEADERS FOR MINISTRY.

"...TO EQUIP HIS PEOPLE FOR WORKS OF SERVICE,
SO THAT THE BODY OF CHRIST MAY BE BUILT UP."

EPHESIANS 4:12

God has called us to ministry. But it's not enough to have a vision for ministry if you don't have the practical skills for it. Nor is it enough to do the work of ministry if what you do is headed in the wrong direction. We need both vision *and* expertise for effective ministry. We need *praxis*.

Praxis puts theory into practice. It brings cutting-edge ministry expertise from visionary practitioners. You'll find sound biblical and theological foundations for ministry in the real world, with concrete examples for effective action and pastoral ministry. Praxis books are more than the "how to" – they're also the "why to." And because *being* is every bit as important as *doing*, Praxis attends to the inner life of the leader as well as the outer work of ministry. Feed your soul, and feed your ministry.

If you are called to ministry, you know you can't do it on your own. Let Praxis provide the companions you need to equip God's people for life in the kingdom.

www.ivpress.com/praxis